D1503134

Discover Your Leaderself

Training the Leader Inside You

Anthony Andrews-Speed, Ph.D.

Other Books by Anthony Andrews-Speed, Ph.D.

The Relationship Roller Coaster:
    Riding Out the Ups & Downs

Living, Loving & Laughing:
    A Guide to Self-Awareness

Meditations, Contemplations & Visualizations

Discover Your Leaderself

Training the Leader Inside You

Anthony Andrews-Speed, Ph.D.

Osmyrrah Publishing

Greensboro, North Carolina

Cover Design: Lee Noel

Editorial Coordination: J. Patrick Grace, Grace Associates, Ltd., Huntington, West Virginia

Printed by Bookcrafters, Inc.

Printed in the United States of America.

Library of Congress Catalog Card Number: 96-70425

10 9 8 7 6 5 4 3 2 1

ISBN 0-9638880-2-1

Publisher's Cataloging in Publication
(Prepared by Quality Books Inc.)

Andrews-Speed, Anthony
    Discover your leaderself : training the leader inside you /
    Anthony Andrews-Speed
        p. cm.
    Includes index.
    Preassigned LCCN: 96-70425
    ISBN 0-9638880-2-1

    1. Leadership. 2. Interpersonal relations. 3. Success.   I.
    Title.

HD57.7.A64 1997   303.3'4
                                    QBI96-40389

Osmyrrah Publishing is a division of The Roberts Group, PO Box 10134, Greensboro, North Carolina 27404. Telephone: 910-292-4061. Web site: http://www.editorialservice.com/osmyrrah

Contents

Acknowledgments

I WANT TO GRATEFULLY ACKNOWLEDGE the following persons for their contributions to the creative process this book represents. A special acknowledgment and appreciation is expressed to Susan, my wife, colleague, and co-creator. Through our vigorous dialogues, she helped me hammer out the fundamental principles and processes contained in this book.

A special thanks also goes to my mentor and friend, Dr. James N. Farr, upon whose shoulders I climbed and stood to see this book.

Thanks to Patrick Grace, and Tony and Sherry Roberts, who went above and beyond the call of duty by carefully reviewing and editing this manuscript. Their creativity, perceptiveness, and life experiences can be seen in the flavors and textures of this book.

A special thanks also to Peter Clancy, Jacquie Rogers, Mark Ernsberger, and Cheryl Michaelis, colleagues and special friends whose feedback on the models and processes in this book have added a whole new dimension to them.

Finally, to all the leaders who have engaged with me in the exciting exploration of what it takes to create reliable and predictable followership—business leaders, political leaders, cultural and religious leaders, the parental leaders who led their children, and the children who led their parents—thank you for teaching me about what works and what doesn't work in the real world of leadership followership. We teach what we most need to learn, and you have been excellent, inspired, and compassionate leaders. Thank you from a grateful follower.

Tapping Your Leaderself

LEADERSHIP ESSENTIALLY INVOLVES three processes executed by the leader. In the first process, the leader interacts with a follower in such a way that the leader can reliably predict that follower's future behavior—not only tomorrow but in a year, three years, even five years from now.

In the second process, the leader interacts with the follower in such a way that the leader can reliably get the follower to follow him or her. Using his leadership skills, the leader elicits the desired and expected response from his followers.

The third process that defines leadership is integrity. Does the leader's behavior—both public and private—fit in with what is considered ethical, moral, and legal in the group, organization, or culture? An individual who has many followers, who can reliably predict future followership behavior, and who can reliably influence that followership behavior, but who leads his followers into followership behavior that is illegal, unethical, or immoral is a failure as a leader.

In this book, you will learn how to tap your "Leader-self"—to lead out of your best qualities and not your worst ones. Your Leaderself is eager to grow and to help others grow—because that is the key to your company's growth.

Also in this book we'll look at different leadership styles. Historic, "old school" leadership is the traditional/autocratic style. The traditional leadership style is defined as one person/party rule. The motto of the old school leader is "command and control." Old school leadership produces short-term efficiencies, quick decision making, and nimble problem solving thanks to centralized decision making and a strong dependence of the followers on the leader. It emphasizes structure, form, and discipline of self and others. It sees productivity in terms of task, product, or service. The power is centralized in the leader, and the leader's primary leadership task is to accumulate more power.

The disadvantage of the traditional/autocratic leadership style is that it tends to stifle the imagination and creativity of the followers, because the leader simply desires that the followers follow in a "lock step" manner. The leader tends to trigger attack and/or avoidance behavior on the part of followers and to reward conformist behavior of followers.

Frequently, the traditional leader will employ the "mushroom theory of leadership," which stipulates that the leader should keep the followers in the dark and feed them business babble (mushrooms adore the dark and survive well on, what would seem to some plants, insubstantial nourishment). The traditional leader frequently engages in blame avoidance—letting others take the heat for his mistakes and errors.

While the traditional leader defers up, controls down, and competes laterally, the participative leader tends to defer down, control up, and cooperate laterally. The operational definition of the participative or team-oriented leader is two or more person/party rule; the real power is split between at least two people or two groups, thus resulting in a system of checks and balances in the use of power.

The motto of the participative/team oriented leader is "train 'em up." The advantage of the participative leadership system is a thorough examination of decisions and problems that allows, and in some cases, forces the followers to be involved in decision making. Thus, there frequently is a much better and more widespread examination of problems; this results in group decisions that produce long-term efficiencies. The participative leader brings differences and conflicts to the surface and resolves them, unlike the traditional leader who tends to suppress divisiveness and conflict, driving it underground and creating cliques and power struggles. Participative leaders prefer to use praise and encouragement as opposed to traditional leaders who tend to use money and status as rewards.

While the traditional leader focuses on tasks and getting the job done, the participative leader centers on getting the most out of his or her followers. Thus, the participatives tend to empower their followers to a significantly greater degree than the traditional leaders. There tends to be a strong dependence on each other and, therefore, more of the follower's personal/interpersonal needs are met within the work environment and through the "informal organization."

Participative leaders often are more open and direct

in sharing their strengths and weaknesses with others. While the traditional leader emphasizes discipline, structure, and form, the participative leader stresses caring, consideration, and fairness. While the traditional leader tends to see productivity in terms of task, product, or service, the participative leader tends to see productivity in terms of people and processes.

The disadvantage of the participative leadership style is that because the participative leader tends to be more "permissive" than the traditional leader, it gives the follower greater possibilities for engaging in passive behavior. Since the participative leader, through a sense of fairness, wants to treat all followers similarly, the individual initiative, ambition, and drive of high performers may be stifled. While the traditional leader style can be overly adversarial, the participative environment can be overly chaotic. With participative leaders attempting to empower followers by allowing them greater participation in decision making, group meetings can be long, boring, inefficient and, in general, a huge waste of time and energy.

There is a Leaderself in every leader—both traditional and participative. The Leaderself is that state of awareness that the leader ideally operates out of when he or she is in their leadership role. The leader is coming from his or her Leaderself when the leader is anchored in the best personality qualities that that person possesses. Thus, for the traditional leader, when that person is operating out of the personality qualities most prevalent or most dominant for traditional leaders—such as being efficient, forceful, organized, and rational—then that leader is operating out of his or her Leaderself.

When the participative leader is operating out of his or

her most prevalent personality qualities—such as conscientious, appreciative, considerate, cooperative, and interpersonally sensitive—then that participative leader is operating out of his or her Leaderself.

The leader is operating out of his or her Stress-self when he or she is operating out of that state of awareness that is coming from the worst qualities and characteristics of that person. The biggest obstacle you have to powerful, flexible, and effective leadership is your Stress-self. Your Stress-self is that state of awareness that stops your Leaderself from operating from the best of the leader. The traditional leader is coming from his or her Stress-self when he or she is argumentative, arrogant, sarcastic, faultfinding, hard-hearted, and hostile. The participative leader is coming from the Stress-self when he or she comes from the worst qualities he or she possesses: being anxious, complaining, dependent, passive/aggressive, and temperamental.

What distinguishes this leadership book from all the other leadership books on your bookshelf? *Discover Your Leaderself* looks at leadership and followership from the perspective of the human system. There are two elements of the human system, and both of these elements or processes must be mastered by the leader to be successful in his or her leadership role. The most important process for the leader to master is the process of his or her own self-awareness. Successful leadership, from this book's perspective, does not depend upon how intelligent the person is, how creative the person is, how eloquent the person is, how clearly the person can articulate his vision, how much value added he contributes to the stockholders, the employees, or the community. It is not a function of whether the leader is task-oriented or people-oriented or has a good balance between task and people orientations. From this book's perspective, leadership is not a function of all the qualities, elements, talents, and abilities that one reads about in other leadership books or hears about on television.

From this book's perspective, successful leadership is a function of the leader mastering his intrapersonal leadership process. Intra means "within." Intrapersonal means "within the skin." The intrapersonal leadership process is the process of awareness within the individual that is managed by the individual. How well the leader manages this internal process of self-awareness is directly correlated with how well the leader leads himself or herself. The single most important element in successful *inter*personal leadership—leading others—is successful *intra*personal leadership—leading one's self. How well one leads one's self is directly correlated with how self-aware one is—how aware one is of one's own inner awareness processes.

There are two intrapersonal leadership processes that the leader needs to be aware of and master. One is an awareness of the best of that leader, what I call the person's Leaderself. You must be aware of, and optimize, your best personality qualities and characteristics. Successful leaders want to optimize whatever Mother Nature bestowed upon them in terms of qualities of character and personality and mind, body, and emotional resources.

However, this is not the most important intrapersonal leadership process. Far more important is being aware of and mastering the worst of one's self—those qualities and characteristics of personality, character, mind, body, and emotions that encourage and enable the leader to engage in horrible, destructive, and cruel behaviors.

Tapping Your Leaderself

Unlike many other leadership books, *Discover Your Leaderself* explores, in depth, the dark side of leadership, which includes the dark side of what it means to be human. Not only does it explore the dark side of human beings and of leadership, it also describes in detail exactly and precisely what the leader needs to do prior to any leadership action to move from the worst of that leader to the best, to move from the worst personality qualities and characteristics of the leader to the best qualities and characteristics of the leader.

In other words, what is the human systems technology the leader can use prior to a leadership action to move from the leader's Stress-self (the worst of him or her) to that leader's Leaderself (the best of him or her)? Models and concepts are provided in the text for discovering and becoming aware of the best and the worst of the leader.

If you are willing to study, learn, and apply the principles and practices of this book, you will encounter breakthrough learning in the following areas:

- You will discover the best of yourself and the worst, especially those parts of the best of you and the worst of you that you are unaware of.

- You will learn your own personal path to go from the worst (the fears, hurts, angers, frustrations, and resentments) to the best (the compassion, power, love, and joy).

- You will learn how to walk that path by using tried and true techniques and practices.

In learning how to become aware of the best and the worst of yourself and how to move from the black pit to the mountaintop, you also will learn how to become aware of the best and the worst of your followers—and you will learn how to move your followers from the worst to the best of them in a powerful, compassionate, and charismatic way.

Tony Speed

PART ONE

Meet Your Leaderself

The Best
And The Worst

MANY SELF-STYLED EXPERTS IN LEADERSHIP will tell you that a leader's success depends upon intelligence or creativity or daring. From my perspective, this is wildly off-base. What is more, the success of a leader does not depend upon how technically skilled he or she is. Nor does it depend upon work experience, good or bad habits, education, culture, or professional status.

I believe you will succeed or fail as a leader because of fundamentally two things:

- Your degree of awareness of **who you are** and of **what you can or cannot do** based on your reservoir of values, skills, and experiences.

- How courageously and compassionately you come to terms with **the worst of yourself!**

Surprised? Let's look at each of these two bedrock principles.

Personal Awareness

Being a leader is based upon a person's ability to achieve personal awareness and to *stay aware*. When you are aware, you are focused on what's going on inside of you and how you can *reach* into yourself and draw forth the right words and actions to deal with the situations at hand. For example, you must confront someone at work, say a colleague. You believe this person has been unrealistic in toting up the numbers it will take for your firm to increase sales of your home-based exercise equipment by 15 percent in your region over the next eight months. Your colleague has all his charts and graphs ready and is on the verge of making his presentation to the top brass. You have a choice: Keep your mouth shut and let him lead the company into delusive planning or pipe up and risk provoking a possibly unpleasant squabble. The colleague, let us further imagine, has a monster ego—a strong, "always-be-right" attitude.

The aware person will factor in all the elements of the confrontational equation—your information and insight versus the other person's; your personality and persuasive power versus his; and the need to safeguard the use of scarce resources, such as company advertising and marketing money. I'm *not* going to put words into your mouth and tell you just what you would say. But take a moment now, a little pause from reading this book, and imagine for yourself what you might say to get your egocentric colleague to question his numbers and perhaps

---

So remember: The best and the worst qualities of a leader will trickle down and become role models for followers.

go back to the drawing board or his calculator and refigure his presentation. Close your eyes and put yourself into this confrontation scenario and play it out. The book will be waiting for you when you return.

So, how did you do? Did you get him to listen to your reasoning? Did you manage to work through his initial outburst of temper over having his judgment questioned? Do the two of you still have a good working relationship?

If you managed any or all of the above, you are on the right track. You are aware, and aware that you're aware. You're using your awareness to further personal and company objectives. In a nutshell, this is what leadership is all about.

If you performed badly in your little daydream scenario, take heart. At least you're now aware that you've got work to do, and, if you stay with me through the rest of this book, we'll get a lot of it done.

Facing the Worst of Yourself

I also said that being a leader meant being ready to face up to *the worst of yourself.* What a strange definition of leadership, you probably muttered to yourself. Well, let's explore this point, and I think you'll get the picture and find that it isn't such a strange idea after all.

When you bobble the ball at work or at home, when you are klutzy or careless or forgetful or badly underestimate what it will take to bring a project in under budget and on time, do you realize that it is quite probably your own negatives that are getting in the way? Without becoming overbearingly "down" on yourself, are you able to acknowledge these negatives, apologize for them (if that's what's called for), repair the damage (make amends to wounded co-workers, for example), and go on in a spirit of hope?

This is what Richard Nixon, for instance, was not able to do during the Watergate debacle. He was totally unable to, as Harry Truman preached and did, act responsibly as the man who sat where the buck stopped. He didn't say, "We (meaning my people) screwed things up, or did something illegal, and *I am responsible.* If you want somebody to blame, blame me." Rather, he ducked and hid and looked everywhere possible for scapegoats to take the rap that was rightly his to shoulder.

Nixon's true nature was perhaps best expressed in his assertion to the press, "I am not a crook." Despite his skillful finessing, through Secretary of State Henry Kissinger, of a new political and trade relationship with Communist China and other foreign and domestic policy successes, Richard Nixon is forever marked by the shameful stain of Watergate and an inglorious fall from power. In a word, he was not a true leader because he was incapable of owning up to and taking responsibility for the worst in himself.

Instead, Nixon tried to displace blame, first onto the media ("saying anything to sell newspapers"), then onto John Dean (who "ratted"), and finally onto H.R. Haldeman, John Erlichman, John Mitchell, and the rest of his gang of liars and crooks.

Lyndon Baines Johnson probably will be remembered not as much for his "Great Society" social programs as for his disastrous failure in leadership during the buildup and debacle in Vietnam. The war in Vietnam was in such a bad state that Johnson decided, on this issue alone, to forego seeking a second term.

You never truly know the soul and spirit of a leader until you know how that leader handles the darkest of dark moments. It's not, in other words, how a leader converses with his angels that counts, but how he copes with his demons. The good days—the days a customer places a $200,000 order or the bank agrees to a new expansion loan or *Business Week* gives your company a favorable write-up—are a piece of cake. Measure a leader's worth, rather, by his or her reaction to a competitor swiping 18 percent of the firm's business or the company failing to win an expected contract or the threat of a strike.

Watch especially to see how a leader treats followers when the company is gripped by a crisis. Does the leader act like a tyrant? A rabid dog? A sniveling rabbit? Or does he or she rise above the turbulence of the moment and manage to inspire or rekindle hope and humor? Then you'll know what kind of leader you are following.

Leaders Can Take the Heat

Immature leaders engage in D & D—Denial and Displacement. Such leaders will deny the worst of themselves—their fears, anger, irrationality, or impetuosity—and displace that worst onto someone else, usually onto a follower or followers. In a word, they'll find a scapegoat, an H.R. Haldeman or a John Dean and duck the responsibility for a bad call or the loss of an account.

Mature leaders will own, or take responsibility for, the worst they have inside of them. "Blame me," said Attorney General Janet Reno after the Waco disaster in which close to 100 members of David Koresch's Branch Davidians died in an inferno that followed the federal agents' charge of their stockade. Later, there would be an intense investigation of commanders on the scene and of the behavior of individual agents. In the heat of the disaster, however, the boss stood up and took the hit. That's leadership of the highest caliber.

Why is it important to be a leader who can take the heat? Because maturity or immaturity in a leader will filter down through the ranks and find expression everywhere. If the No. 1 honcho ducks responsibility, probably so will No. 2—and No. 22. If No. 1 is able to accept blame, leaders down the authority lines will be more likely to follow suit. Harry Truman's willingness to have the buck stop with him trained up that same willingness in his followers. Richard Nixon's penchant for suspicion and underhanded tactics elicited similar qualities in H.R. Haldeman, John Erlichman, and Spiro Agnew.

The Buck Stops

Self-responsibility is the willingness of a leader to own the best and the worst of him. It is the willingness of the leader to take personal responsibility for not only his strengths, powers, abilities, and skills, but more importantly, his weaknesses, sins, fears, angers, and hurts.

A Nation of Pointing Fingers

Today we see a great number of immature leaders in this country. The Democrats tend to blame social ills on the Republicans, and the Republicans on the Democrats. A president may blame his failure of leadership on "a gridlocked Congress." Congress (especially if it's led by an opposition party) will saddle the president with blame for unresolved problems.

It goes further than that. Religious zealots will blame atheists, agnostics, and the non-churchgoing for society's moral slippage. Secular humanists lambast the religiously fervent for trying to force-feed narrow-minded, pietistic morality to a body public. People of means will tend to suspect the poor of a lack of gumption or willingness to work. The poor talk of being exploited by the rich (the very stuff of Marxism!). The result is a massive and seemingly endless dance of denial.

With denial comes, almost always, displacement. The scapegoating leader maneuvers the blame; he or she transfers it to subordinates—or any other outsiders possible. This only propels the followers to do the same, passing the buck on down the line and ducking out on their responsibilities in the same way they see old No. 1 doing. Followers, you see, typically will do a marvelous job of following the leader.

Immature anger is anger that a leader has but pretends is provoked by a follower (*"You* make me mad," or *"You* caused me to foul things up").

Mature anger is what I call "charismatic power." The aware leader will use such anger not to empower himself but to empower the follower.

Meet Your Leaderself

The best of you is your Leaderself. This self contains all your strengths, your positives, the qualities that will bring out the best in your followers.

It is important that you recognize who your Leaderself is—what it's made of. What are your best qualities? Are you forceful, efficient, and organized? Or are you considerate, conscientious, and cooperative? Both operate out of the Leaderself, depending on the person.

The key is to be aware of the best of you, to be willing to meet your Leaderself. The Leaderself is a state of awareness. How well the leader manages this internal process of self-awareness is directly correlated with how well the leader leads himself or herself. The single most important element in successfully leading others is, first, successfully leading your self. How well you lead your self is directly related to how self-aware you are—how well you know your Leaderself.

C H A P T E R   T W O

Where Do Leaders Come From?

SO HOW DID YOU START OUT? Your parents contributed genetic coding. The blood flowing through your veins reaches back through your parents, your grandparents, back all the way to Adam and Eve. But do you know what all that genetic coding really amounts to? A lot of potential. When you made your grand entrance at birth—alive and kicking—all you really knew was that you had survived.

Then, immediately, you started having experiences. Your tiny body whooshed forth, sliding from that nice warm, wet chamber into a world of blinding light and blaring noise. Somebody spanked you, and you hadn't even pulled any pranks yet. Then hands put, ugh!,*clothes!* on your bottom. You were washed, weighed, and whisked off down the hospital hall to be deposited in a bed next to a dozen other new arrivals.

Hey, you, kid in the next bed, pipe down, will ya? I need to catch up on some sleep!

Experiences. One after another. And what did your

mind do, automatically? It made recordings of them. Deeply grooved. Indestructible.

Your mind filed those recordings in one of two categories: "me" and "not me."

Whatever you caught yourself thinking or feeling, whatever anybody did that had a direct impact on you and caused a feeling, got to be known as "me." This is who I am, the guy or the gal who is having these thoughts or these feelings. And those feelings and thoughts gave rise to what I call your "meaning."

Your "meaning map" is composed of your perceptions of what is true and real for you, in a particular situation. Each person's subjective meaning map is different and unique. This subjective meaning map can be contrasted with an objective meaning map. Here's an example: For an individual, the objective meaning map is that there

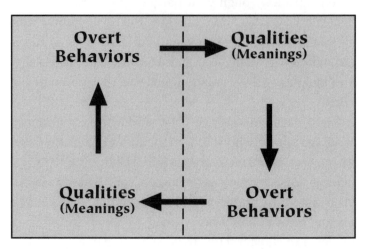

Person 1   **Person 2**

MEANING MAP

Person 1 does something. Person 2 gives a meaning to Person 1's actions and reacts. Person 1 places a meaning on Person 2's reaction and responds. Meaning, response, meaning, response, and so it goes.

was a meeting of supervisors on Monday. However, each individual in that meeting applied his or her own set of subjective "meanings" and determined that the meeting was a "good meeting" or a "bad meeting."

The "Me," "Not Me" Recordings

Other experiences went down as "not me." Your mom and your dad, for example, quickly became the god and the goddess of your little universe. They were towering figures and had overriding influence.

If you were afraid of the dark and you cried, Mom came and held you and sang lullabies. The experience went down on your meaning map. What registered was: Crying gets me solace, protection, a savior. Or perhaps you recorded that Mom didn't come. And you stayed afraid. Perhaps a loneliness or an emptiness set in. Or maybe you took it differently and learned to be more self-reliant. Whatever it was, it became—and still is—a part of you.

Your Board of Directors

How do you make decisions about everything from corporate mergers to what you'll have for dinner? You consult your "Board of Directors." Your Board of Directors or "family within" is a set of personalities developed from your experiences of the important people in your life— or the personality qualities of those key people.

Your mother or father are the first people to go on your Board of Directors. If, as a child, you experienced Mom as open, loving, and caring, then you may have created a "Loving Mom" as part of your Board of Directors. Another side of Mom might have been critical, anxious, and fear-ridden. That part likewise became part of the Board, as did your strong, silent Dad or your angry, distant Dad.

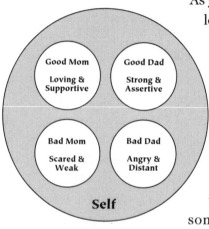

As you go through childhood, adolescence, and early adulthood, you keep adding to your Board of Directors—a powerful aunt, a charismatic teacher, a cantankerous grandfather.

Obviously, the members of your Board are not cut from the same cloth. Among themselves, they are quarrelsome and frequently at odds. There are shifting alliances. Compromises. Pacts sealed, and pacts broken.

The principal figures on your Board, however, basically are "good Mom" and "bad Mom," then "good Dad" and "bad Dad." They are the ones behind the hard wiring of your interior system—how you are going to experience love, hate, joy, sadness, peace, fear, hilarity, anger, gentleness, rage.

What we do in our adult lives—our behavior in the work world, whether we are leaders or followers or (quite likely for many readers) both—is a playing out of the strategies we learned from Mom and Dad, as signified by our Board of Directors, for responding to situations in our growing up.

We Unconsciously Compare Everyone We Meet to Our Tapes

As human beings, we constantly are bombarded by external waves of stimulation such as sound waves, light waves, and pressure waves. These waves impact upon a whole set of "tapes" or "prerecorded programs" stored in our mental and emotional equipment. Each of us has a little inspector figure standing inside us with a clipboard, ready to check off each experience we have as corresponding to something already in our memory bank.

For example, when I look at Charlotte, that white-haired lady in the corner workstation who always wears pink lipstick and gold earrings, I see . . . my Aunt Harriet. (That "seeing," of course, is the result of light waves bursting through my optical lenses and getting translated into images by my brain.) And Mom never seemed to cotton much to Aunt Harriet. Mom thought she was a chatterbox and a busybody. Truthfully, though, Charlotte really *does* talk a lot. (Sound waves!) And I'm *sure* she has been trying to delve into my life.

Since Mom was the first female I ran into and since she had so much power in my life, I naturally will tend to see anybody or any experience through the prism of all those recordings I made of Mom and how she reacted to things.

The other powerful prism, of course, is my files of memories (or tapes) of my father. So when a new hire comes into my department at work and is introduced as "Don," immediately my tapes start clicking. Don is a male and that automatically puts him into the "Dad memories" category. Next, I notice that Don has graying hair parted on the right side. Just like Dad's! I also see that he has metal-rimmed glasses and brown eyes. Well, Dad had those, too!

Suddenly I get a strong feeling that I'm not going to get along too well with this "Don" guy. He sure looks an awful lot like my Dad, and Dad, after all, was one mean

The Comparison Game

Who are these human beings that you create as your enemies? These enemies are anybody who isn't like you. This is an interesting trap, since no one in the world is like you. Ultimately, you are the only you that will ever be. Still we all play the comparison game.

Contained in your mind is a checklist of the way things and people "should be." This checklist was developed by your mind as a function of your personal history, as part of the training and conditioning you received in the process of growing up. You developed the checklist out of your need to say, feel, and do those things that would enhance your survival odds. You do not say, feel, or do those things that would be a threat to your survival. Therefore, whatever fits or agrees with your checklist is right, good, and true; whatever is different from or disagrees with your checklist is bad, evil, or untrue.

guy. Always hurting me with words or that big black belt. I didn't have too many light and carefree moments with my father, nosiree, and I can see right now that it's going to be the same way with Don.

Only I won't realize where my negative feelings about Don are coming from! Just as I didn't understand why I thought Charlotte was going to be a bother. In fact, I will make up reasons for my likes and dislikes that often have nothing *at all* to do with the true source of those reactions.

I'll tell myself—and my confidantes—that I don't trust Charlotte because she talks with a funny accent, and so, she's not "one of us." Or that Don gets on my nerves because he seems to be a know-it-all and is always flaunting the prestigious college he attended. But those aren't the real reasons for my negative feelings about these two people.

Our Hidden Tapes

After birth, we began to get buried under a pile of "do this" and "don't do that" or even "don't be this or that" kind of tapes. Those tapes are heaped on us by the various sides of Mom and Dad on our Board, and by certain other highly significant others during our formative years.

To a great extent, all these caveats—"do's" and "don'ts" and "thou shalt nots"—virtually eclipse our underlying self. They shape our beliefs, our ethics, and our actions. After awhile, we simply think of ourselves (in our unawareness) as a collection of tapes or programs.

These tapes are the sources of all our "isms": sexism, racism, even nationalism. We identify and feel comfortable with people who are "like us"—and that means "like what we grew up with" (i.e. our Board of Directors). We categorize those who fall outside our checklist of acceptable traits, looks, or ways of speaking or behaving as "foreigners." And how can we possibly trust someone we don't even know?

So these hidden tapes, these indelibly etched-in, compulsive programs, are often what drive our beliefs, thoughts, and actions on the job. We think we're the captain of our own ship, but let me say it loud and clear, nine times out of ten, we aren't in charge! The tapes, which collectively compose the qualities of the members, are. It's the tapes that are piloting our ship.

That means you end up being run by a part of you that you don't even know you have. Not only that, but these well-masked tapes play out your fears, anxieties, and residual anger, against similar feelings sparked by other people's life-experience tapes. No wonder we find ourselves engaged in so many clashes, many of which seem patently irrational.

Anger Learned Becomes Anger Lived

If you grew up in a family where there were high levels of fear, I'll guarantee you there were also high levels of anger. Anger is the other side of the same coin: Where there is fear, there is anger, and vice versa.

If a person grows up in an environment in which the norm is explosive anger or expressions of hatred or abuse, that person will be dysfunctional. Essentially, you were raised in an emotional war zone. In your psyche, in your skin, you looked around and experienced Mom and Dad, aunts and uncles, siblings and cousins, as physiologically dumping out high levels of stress hormones.

When people plunge into either anger or fear or sadness or hurt, they are going into stress. That was true when you were a child, and it's still true for you—and everybody else—at home and at work.

Lower levels of fear in the home produce not panic but rather anxiety, apprehension, guilt, shame, and edginess. Lower levels of anger will manifest as frustration, impatience, and nitpicking.

Whether the levels at home were high, moderate, or low, however, they will be reflected in your adult self—and on the job.

People who were abused as children—made to feel either fear or anger or both—typically will imagine themselves as being abused in a group dynamic (whether or not this is actually the case). Such individuals will let themselves be nudged into their "abused self" (a

> **You Have a Choice**
>
> *≋ The trap is you think that you can choose not to be angry. But the more you choose not to be angry, the more angry you're going to get. That's not a choice. You can't choose a "not." It is in choosing to be nurturing, caring, sensitive, open, powerful, and compassionate that you grow. Choose to grow up those parts.*

subcomponent of the Stress-self which we will discuss later) and will react accordingly. They will become either explosive in striking back, carping, or passive aggressive (assuming smoldering, hostile silences, for example).

Traditionally, autocratic leadership says get rid of such people. Fire them; get them off the team. Or you move them to some place in the organization where they won't be as disruptive.

In the new team-oriented leadership matrix, such responses generally are discouraged. They're a sign of poor leadership. For example, if I am the CEO of a conglomerate and I have on board an investment banker who grew up in an anger-filled environment and who is inappropriately expressing anger in front of my team, my impulse when he explodes for the umpteenth time is to fire him. However, my hotheaded executive is bringing in $20 million a year for the firm. Somehow, I must *lead* this person into becoming a good team player. What do I do?

Call Upon Your Leaderself

Before I can lead *him*, I must first learn how to lead

Locked in by the Age of Ten

A fellow named Sigmund Freud said that, by the age of six, you have most of your significant negative experiences and most of your significant losses. You've got those laid down in tracks on your personality tapes. They are your Stress-self.

Somewhere between the ages of six and ten, your Stress-self is formed, and your personality builds up around it. The way to survive is to use the machinery in your head.

So by age ten, you have some significant negative decisions locked in, and you are doing your best to defend against them. Then you end up later in life playing out those patterns that you evolved in order to protect yourself from going through the hurt that you thought back then, in your childlike mind, was going to kill you.

myself into my center. If I can be centered, focused, and calm in the eye of a hurricane, I will be ready to decide what to do about him. I will need to use my power centering to deal with a shark as a shark and coach this executive into rechanneling his anger in a way that will serve his purpose as well as the group's purpose. This may involve putting him through a leadership impact study so that he can see how his anger is affecting others negatively. It also may mean sending him to self-awareness workshops or counseling. And most of all, it may require patience, both on the part of the angry executive and his peers.

Every other member of the team who has a problem with this person's anger, in fact, will need to be "trained up" to be able to cope productively with emotions unleashed in meetings and in personal interactions.

Since there is a huge quantity of overly angry individuals in business, the issue of identifying and rechanneling anger is real and important. Left untended, anger builds to explosive pitch or else turns subtly poisonous. Either outcome can spell doom for an organization.

Even more common than the problem of the explosive executive is that of the hypercritical naysayer. This stance is likely the result of lower levels of anger or fear experienced in childhood. Such types are almost invariably negative about everything: "I don't think we can do that," or "Not much chance that'll work."

The principle is exactly the same. How can you take what this individual is doing and use it to serve your purpose and that of the whole organization?

When I was in college, my fraternity had what we called "the hot poop counselor." His job was to disagree with whatever was advocated by others and to advocate what other members thought was unrealistic. This worked out well. Thanks to the hot poop counselor, we always had the opportunity for a deeper dialogue on the issues, whether to plan this or that event, vote in or vote down this or that pledge, spend money on something or not.

Companies need such critical feedback, too, at all levels and in regard to all substantive decisions.

The genuine value of the naysayers is that they can often see the downside to a course of action. Instead of rejecting the naysayer's opinion, welcome it as a prod to

---

The obvious is that which is never seen until someone expresses it simply.

—Kahlil Gibran

Predicting the Future

 The best predictor of future patterns is past patterns.

Children learn to

Think

Mom and Dad's thoughts,

Do

Mom and Dad's actions,

Feel

Mom and Dad's feelings.

Learn what Mom and Dad live

and then

live what they learn.

deeper research. You may really need more information than you currently have. The outcome of listening to the naysayers is that you probably will be much more fully aware of what the strengths and the weaknesses are of a given approach or course. As a leader, you want *both* sides of the picture—the light side and the dark side.

CHAPTER   THREE

Why Do Leaders Act The Way They Do?

You take it in as a child.
You put it out as an adult.
You take it in as a son.
You put it out as a father and husband.
You take it in as a daughter.
You put it out as a mother and wife.
You take it in as a follower.
You put it out as a leader.

LEADERS WILL DO TO THE ORGANIZATION what they experienced being done to them by their family members, primarily their parents. Leaders will express both the best and the worst of their family members onto their followers. And followers will express both the best and the worst of their family members onto their leaders (and their followers).

The structure of the organization will fit the structure of the chief executive's personality. The leader will successfully lead others in direct proportion to how successfully he or she leads himself or herself. When the leader moves into and expresses the best of himself or herself, the majority of the followers will move into and express the best of themselves. Likewise, when the leader moves into and expresses the worst of himself or herself, the majority of the followers will express the worst of themselves. The way the CEO treats his followers is the way the followers will treat their followers/customers.

The Family Business

All businesses are family businesses. Leaders and followers structure their professional relationships based on the personal values they learned from their families. To see your leadership through the eyes of your followers, observe how you felt about the leadership of your parents (focus primarily on your same-sex parent). The leader and the follower in their experience create the group/team/organization as their family and create the members of the organization as members of their family. Over time, they will attribute personality qualities of members of their family to members of the group/team/organization.

Voices, Visions & Feelings

Skillful, contemporary leadership requires that the leader be aware of and *fluent* in at least three languages: verbal brain language, visual brain language, and feeling brain language.

Verbal Brain Language

Book or word people organize their experiences into voices, words, and numbers. They are experts in deductive logic, see business as a "numbers game," and are bottom line or profit oriented.

The voices have to do with *thinking* and come out of the verbal brain. It's through these voices that the brain organizes raw sensory awareness (sound waves, pressure waves, light waves) into words and numbers.

Most people who go into business are verbal brainers—thinkers and analyzers. They are good at articulating principles and policy, writing mission statements, drafting memos and speeches.

Visual Brain Language

Although verbal brainers have tended, up until now, to occupy most of the management positions, they are not nearly as potent for leadership as are visual brainers, who excel at having visions. They organize experiences into pictures, sometimes even motion pictures. Under the inspiration of their vision, they are ready to move out and conquer the world.

Many political and business units have moved to a preference for right-brain visualizing. Instead of mission statements, visual brainers think in terms of organizational visions or pictures. The picture may signal unity or harmony or teamwork or energy.

Though verbal brainers have tended to dominate business, we are currently in a process of transition. Visual brainers are really coming to the fore.

Feeling Brain Language

People also speak through the language of feelings. In every business environment, there are emotional and physical feelers.

Emotional feelers are people of the heart; they organize experiences into feelings (happy, angry, sad). These people/relationship oriented folks see business as a morality play. They are extremely team leadership oriented.

Physical feelers or sensors are people of the deed or act. They organize experiences into sensations (pleasure, pain, movement). They see business as an athletic performance and are action/performance/task oriented.

The verbal brain language is the language at which managers are most skillful. Next is the visual brain language. Leaders most need to learn and understand feeling brain language.

Handling Emotional Feelers

There are huge numbers of emotional feelers coming into the business world today. So it's extremely important for all who aspire to leadership to recognize them and learn how best to deal with them. This is truly part of the leadership challenge of our times.

In the old days, verbal brainers drove emotional feelers out of the organization. It wasn't really malicious; it's just the way things were. Business was about cold hard numbers on the one hand and about "charging the hill" to "get the job done" on the other. The two modes were totally complementary. Anybody who had strong "feelings" about something was judged to be "getting in the way."

If the emotional feelers stayed in the organization at all, they went underground and engaged in guerrilla warfare. Passive aggression. They would get to the boss by stressing him into a heart attack.

Today's emotional feelers work for the quality of the relationships on the job. They are high on "atmosphere" or "ambiance." They're in there pitching because they want to experience positive human rewards, not because they want to make a million bucks.

All this is fine, so long as managers learn how to identify feelers and respond to them, meet them "where they live." It's terribly difficult to get people to follow you if you're talking number-cruncher language and they're waiting for you to show them you have a beating heart. If they perceive you as all head and no heart, you as the leader are sunk. They're *not* going to follow you.

Being fluent in the language of the mid-brain—the language of feelings—is where most leaders fail.

The hardest thing to grasp is what's in the pit of your stomach. Those are your feelings, physical and emotional.

And guess what is the number one thing that will stop upward movement of a promising individual in any organization? Will stop his or her career cold?

Anger!

What Harvey Levinson, Harvard psychologist and founder of the Levinson Institute, has called "the abrasive personality," all too common in business, is the hard-charging, comin'-right-at-ya, "let's-get-the-job-done" aggressive, task-oriented climber. As this person is moving

Use It or Lose It

〜*The brain is much like a muscle: use it or lose it. There are 95-year-old men and women who could run circles around us in terms of their intellectual capabilities. For example, in his final years on the tour, tennis pro Jimmy Conners would run circles around the whippersnappers on the tennis court—by using his brain. Conners started out slowly, but once he got all greased up, he could often go for five sets. While young tennis players were burning out and getting flustered, savvy Conners used his brain more than his body to extend his career.*

up through the lower echelons of an organization, the powers that be look down and say, "This is great! Look at that Tom go!" Or, "What a terrific worker that Marybeth is! Wow! She can do it all!"

However, by the time the climbers approach the level of upper middle management, they have left so many bodies in their wake and ticked off so many colleagues and subordinates, the senior people will be inclined to say, "I don't want to have to work with that person." The top people, you see, have long since discovered that the only way to get anything accomplished at that level is to work together cooperatively.

So Tom and Marybeth's upward movement comes to a halt. They are bright and creative and tigers of energy. But they also are loose cannons—hostile and unforgiving of others' mistakes.

By the way, Tom and Marybeth won't recognize that they're angry. They really don't see it that way. To them, they're only "getting the job done," right?

Since, historically, this angry, aggressive style has been the one that's been the most successful, today's organizations are in a period of lagging adjustment to the new realities.

Positive, creative leadership requires developing the Leaderself. The Leaderself is that state of awareness that you ideally operate out of when you are in your leadership role. The Leaderself can learn, develop, and grow by developing fluency and skill with the three languages, especially the feeling brain language.

The Mid-Brain/Feeling Brain's Language

The language of the mid-brain, the third language that we all speak, is the most powerful language that human beings can express. It also happens to be the most powerful language in terms of relationships and, consequently, in terms of leadership. I call this the language of the mid-brain, because that is, primarily, where it is mediated.

The language of the mid-brain is *feelings*.

There are two kinds of feelings: physical feelings, which we can call "sensations," and emotional feelings, which are more like waves welling up inside or washing over us.

Being in touch with physical feelings is like being Michael Jordan flying through the air en route to a slam dunk. It is being part of something that is focused and flowing toward an attainable goal.

People who are *not* in touch with their feelings need help. They are the walking, or the sleepwalking, dead. (A tragically high percentage of human beings go through life like this, and if they are trying to be leaders, it's a real slog, believe me, both for them and for the people who allegedly follow them.)

In Chapter Seven, Centering Yourself, I list a number of peaceful and powerful way techniques and strategies that also can be used to help get in touch with one's feelings.

Broad Categories of Behavior

All human behavior (my behavior, yours, or your mother-in-law's...anybody's) falls into one of three broad categories: positive outcomes, negative outcomes, and neutral outcomes. Outcomes are how a person ends up feeling as a result of playing out a behavior pattern.

> *From sensations → emotions*
> *From emotions → visions*
> *From visions → voices*
> *From voices → actions*
> *From actions → sensations*
> *from sensations . . .*

THE DEVELOPMENT OF YOUR BOARD OF DIRECTORS

How do human beings end up with the personalities they have? Personalities are composed of physical feelings, emotional feelings, visions, and voices. Our actions are the result of a cycle of sensations, emotions, visions, and voices. The leader must be fluent in all of these "languages" to influence behavior—or, in short, to lead.

Positive Behaviors or Your Act

The first of these categories groups all the positive experiences you had as a child. Whenever you did something and ended up feeling good, self-assured, respected, even glowing, you filed away the experience into a catchall folder. Out of this folder you came to develop what I term *your act.*

Your act is what you put together so other people would accept you. Maybe even love you. In any case, they would give you enough positive feedback to make you think that maybe, just maybe, you had a place in the universal scheme of things, that your existence was more than a fluke.

For some people, their act is about being loving, caring, and warmhearted. For others, it may be being conscientious and responsible. Still others may put together an act that manifests as happy-go-lucky, life-of-the party, anything that other people are likely to enjoy and find worthwhile.

If you want to know more precisely what your act is, ask your spouse to tell you why he or she was attracted

How Do You Know You're a Leader?

🖝 *Many people think they're leaders just because they're a warm body in some position of authority. And like drum majors with the big hats and the waving batons, they march down Main Street thinking they're creating the strong, driving sound.*

The first clue they have that they are not leaders is when they march down Main Street but the band turns on Third. As the music fades in the distance, the self-described leaders scramble to catch up, to get in front of the group again.

Such scramblers are not leaders.

Remember, needs drive behavior. People will be induced to follow you if they think that by doing so they get their needs met.

to you in the first place.

Nothing personal, but you were not born being witty or generous or responsible, or whatever your particular act happens to be. You developed yourself that way to orchestrate a certain kind of positive feedback from others "out there" in the world around you.

Negative Behaviors

The second category of behavior patterns are negative outcome patterns. When things went bad for you as a child, when you got in over your head, when you got blamed, scolded, punished, and ridiculed, you scooped up those feelings and memories and stuffed them into a folder labeled "Stress-self."

Much of this had to do with behavior patterns expressed by Mom and Dad in their interactions with each other and you. They would express sentiments such as: "I can't believe you'd do anything so dumb!" "Stop that immediately, you're being a bad boy (or girl)." "You just keep that up and see what it gets you." "Just wait until your father gets home."

Remember: Your primary goal on the outside of the womb is the same as it was on the inside—to survive. To do that, you found you needed points of reference on negative experiences. What did you have to do (or not do) to avoid such-and-such consequences?

Thus, as we grow older, we retain the reflexes contained for us in our Stress-self folder. We operate our lives, first of all, out of a lot of unidentified avoidance needs. And, secondly, when we do run into painful situations, such as when colleagues or others become critical of us, we will dip into our negative folder for an "appropriate" reaction. In other words, we will act very much in our adult life as we did when we were children. The emotion simply gets channeled through an adult prism, that's all. (See "Transformational Process of Your Board of Directors" on Page 56.)

Meet Your Stress-self

The worst of you is what I call your *Stress-self.* This is the self which, if let go unrestrained, will tear up your organization, your systems, your hopes and goals, your followers, and yourself along with it.

Everyone has a Stress-self. You are not "a bad person" simply because you get nervous, anxious, frustrated, or resentful. The next person may not have your negative qualities, but he or she will have others that are potentially just as destructive.

We do need to master our Stress-self, to tame it and tone down its rough edges. The more we know about this self, the better we'll be able to recognize it when it manifests itself and the more likely we'll be able to control it, instead of allowing it, like a runaway demon, to take charge of us.

In the leader-follower dance, the trick, if you are the leader, is to express the best qualities *of your followers* in your own overt behavior. This is what they will *really* resonate to and appreciate you for. In other words, if your followers value precision, be as precise as possible. If they are high on warmth in interpersonal relations, be warm.

This reflection of best followers' qualities is especially important on occasions when the followers are expressing their *worst* qualities. Let's say, for instance, that you run a small management consulting agency and your followers' worst tendency is to waste time (over-describe everything, complicate things, give peripheral tasks higher priority than the main tasks). How can you get them to discipline themselves to be more efficient? By identifying their *best* quality and reflecting it back to them, that's how. Perhaps their best quality is drive, that combination of energy and focus that helps us go out and do what we have to do, and even relish the doing of it.

"Let's bear down on identifying ways that we make less than efficient use of our time," you might suggest. Lead them into a brainstorming session. In all probability,

---

The biggest obstacle to powerful, flexible changes is your Stress-self. Your Stress-self is that state of awareness that stops your Leaderself from operating from a powerful, effective, sensitive state. Your Stress-self blinds, deafens, and depotentiates your Leaderself. The Stress-self is also the part of you of whom you are least aware.

they will come up with many of the things that are slowing down your operation—perhaps even a few items you hadn't thought of yourself. Because you made the problem into a project that plugged into their penchant for "drive," you're halfway home toward solving your quandary. And whatever points your followers do not manage to surface in the brainstorming session, you'll be able to raise yourself. Even better, you'll be raising such points in an atmosphere of dynamic focus and willingness on the followers' part to make improvements.

Living in the Comfort Zone

In the womb, it was wonderful. Heaven. On a scale of one to ten, I'd say the in-womb life is, normally, a plus-ten experience.

Then you are born and you shoot down to minus ten. Separation anxiety. Besides, there are people poking and prodding you. All sorts of bad stuff is happening. You go from heaven to hell. Dante's inferno.

When we start experiencing emotional pain, we react by creating a wall. We literally wall out the pain. Actually, we create a box, a wall that goes all around us on four sides.

Once that box is in place, all that is available for you to experience is what you have inside those four walls. The closer those walls are to your center of being, the narrower your range of experience is going to be.

Denial is all about keeping those walls close, sharply limiting the range of emotions you can feel. Feelings that begin to creep outside of this range will make you feel uncomfortable. Unconsciously, you reject those feelings or experiences. Feelings or experiences that take you out of your range—some people call it *the comfort zone*—

will trigger defensive mechanisms to prompt you to quash the feeling or pull back from the experience.

And it's inside of that box, however small you choose to make it, that you live your life. Great fear, self-consciousness, or feelings of inferiority all promote keeping the box small and "secure."

Nonetheless, the part of you that is inside the small box is important. It constitutes your sea of tranquility, your peaceful center. This small center houses your capacities to get along gently with other people, to negotiate compromises in a polite, systematic way, and to experience your own quiet essence.

Breaking Through the Wall

Much of the trauma in the work world comes from interactions with people who challenge your comfort zone. If you are a restrained type, raised in a family where it was taboo to scream or shout, a boss given to bursts of temper and warnings that his subordinates better "shape up" is a threat to your comfort zone.

If your efforts are bent on staying in your little boxed-in comfort zone, you will either have to hunker down and try to ignore your boss or quit and look for another

---

The powerful leader continually works at mastering his or her inner psychological process of being comfortably uncomfortable *in difficult/demanding/stressful leadership situations. Transforming "bad" stress into "good" stress is an essential tool in the kitbag of the powerful leader.*

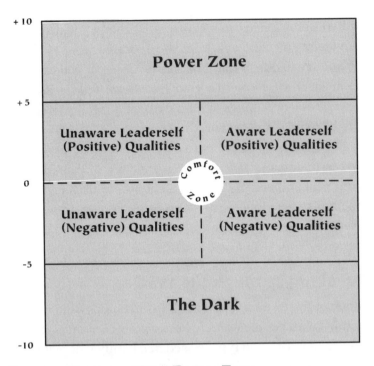

YOUR COMFORT ZONE AND YOUR POWER ZONE

We all live in a comfort zone, a place where we feel safe. Trauma in the work world comes from people and situations that challenge our comfort zones. A leader must become comfortable in the uncomfortable. Power techniques, such as power anchoring, help leaders enter the power zone—where great visions reside. You will experience your most positive qualities at their greatest intensity in the power zone.

job. You certainly won't be able to find it within you to stand up to him.

Leaders face the same problems as everyone else: You leave the shelter of home and sally forth into a work world that is populated with Attilas, sharks, and Darth Vaders. And often you don't have the tools to cope. You may assume a position of powerlessness, or, like some bugs when they are under attack, try to hide or play dead.

What is required in this situation is that you "hit the wall." Direct your self right at the wall you have erected around your center and ram into it in an effort to break through to the other side. Sounds gutsy? It is.

Are you a jogger? Then you probably know what it feels like to "break through" to a place of being comfortable running even though you felt you had no more energy left to burn. You are beyond the strength level you had calculated you had for the run. You are into an afterburner stage.

Imagine going down for a deep-sea dive for the first time. Or jumping out of an airplane with a parachute strapped to your back. Or confronting whitewater rapids in a one-person kayak.

There's a first time for everything, as the saying goes. And so there is, too, a first time for "hitting the wall" of your comfort zone.

To hit the wall means to learn how to be comfortable with the uncomfortable. To get into this domain outside your small box, you will need some power techniques, such as power breathing. We do this in workshops and group experiences. Trained facilitators instruct people on how to breathe deeply, very deeply, in great inner waves of energy until they feel as if they're part of a raging ocean. It's usually kind of scary, but in most cases, participants will hit their wall and break through to the other side.

The physiology of power breathing is instructive. When you engage in any physical activity for long enough, you will find yourself drawing in oxygen and pushing out carbon dioxide. In the process, you will flood the physical feeling part of the brain, mainly the brain stem, the cerebellum, and everything else that controls automatic sensory physiological functions. Then you will activate the limbic system, the hypothalamus. At that point, you will be open to a rush of physical and emotional feelings, washing over you. Both hemispheres of the brain, the right and the left, will be flooded with oxygen, blood, and awareness. The capillaries will dilate.

You will be in a lucid dream state similar to the altered states of consciousness that can be produced by drugs.

Feelings flood up into the area of your brain where you process your raw sensory awareness into voices and visions. Psychologically, you are flying. You are experiencing much of what can be accessed through sensory deprivation or fasting or other ascetic practices. In other words, you are having a powerful mystical experience.

It may seem to some readers as if we have wandered far afield from leadership. We have not. Leaders absolutely need to experience and get comfortable with the rather threatening flooding of feelings that goes with hitting the wall, with breaking through to the unconscious.

The greatest leaders have powerful visions. Where do such visions come from? From their unconscious. How to do they get into their unconscious? By hitting the wall, by breaking through. The dimension they gain access to may be nightmarish, as it was for Hitler, or paradisiacal, as it was for Ghandi. In either case, they will be in touch with strong superhuman currents whirling up from the vortex of our nature. (For ways to turn defense mechanisms into powers through awareness, see "Powers

---

To be a successful leader in a democracy, you must master two psychological processes. You must learn to be comfortably uncomfortable, and you must learn to expand your comfort zone so you are comfortable in a broader, wider, and more varied set of situations.

> **Hotwired**
>
> ∾ *We all have a few things in common: a mind, a body with physical feelings, and emotions. You are unique in the way that you have wired up your mind, your body, and in the way that wiring translates into your behavior. There is no other human being on this planet who has the same wiring that you have.*

of Your Board of Directors" on page 54.)

The Secret of Charisma

Inevitably, in a book about leadership, people expect the author to talk about charisma. The secret of charisma is this: I will see you as charismatic if I feel better *about me* when I'm around you. So if I feel empowered, loving, joyful, and confident; if my self-esteem, my appreciation of life and being goes up, I will do what the shrinks call "projection." I will project all those feelings back to you and experience you as the source of my good feelings. So, without realizing what the process involves, I will call you "charismatic" because now I feel better and I attribute that feeling to your "power." Democrats, for example, thought of President John F. Kennedy as charismatic; Republicans thought of President Ronald Reagan that way.

There's negative charisma, too, let's not forget. Mussolini was charismatic. So were Hitler and Joe Stalin. Their followers felt good about themselves too when they spent time around their heroes. Also those followers started feeling superior to all other people, because when you're following somebody like Mussolini there's only his way and the wrong way. So you, as a follower, get to be "right," while the rest of the world is "wrong."

You can tell much about a person by asking who he or she sees as "charismatic." Because charisma exists within us based on how we structure our perceptions of the world. We "create" other people's charisma out of our own needs and our own values.

I can get many of the same feelings by just being out in a spectacular natural setting, such as the Blue Ridge Mountains, on a glorious autumn day. I'll look at all those brilliant red and gold leaves and I'll feel just terrific—terrific about myself. Just like some people feel being around "charismatic" personalities.

Powers of Your Board of Directors

We use these behaviors to limit our awareness and shrink into our comfort zone. By enhancing our awareness, we can turn these defense mechanisms into powers. For example, an aware leader can use the positive qualities of the act of denial—the tunnel vision or complete centering of self—to focus on a project.

Denial: Not seeing, not hearing, not feeling. Moving sounds (voices) and/or sights (pictures) and/or sensations and/or feelings from the domain of awareness to the domain of unawareness.

Internalization (Introjection): Moving sights (pictures) and/or sounds (voices) and/or sensations and/or feelings that are perceived to be outside one's self to within one's self, generally without conscious awareness.

"Telling Your Truth" (Rationalization): Focusing one set of sounds (voices) and/or sights (pictures) and/or sensations and/or emotions rather than another set of sounds (voices) and/or sights (pictures) and/or sensations and/or emotions, generally without conscious awareness.

Why Do Leaders Act The Way They Do?

Charisma is a feeling and also a state of consciousness. Within this state, I project either good or bad feelings upon another person or upon a scene in nature.

So, in a leadership role, I attempt to use my personality as a mirror for people to look into and find something good, dynamic, and inspiring. But they are really finding it within themselves as they bounce it off me.

Externalization: Moving sights and/or sounds and/or sensations and/or feelings from within one's self to outside one's self, generally without conscious awareness.

Forgetting (Amnesia): Ceasing to be aware of a sight (picture) and/or sound and/or sensation and/or emotion, generally without conscious awareness.

Splitting (Dissociation): Splitting one set of sounds (voices) and/or sights (pictures) and/or sensations and/or emotions into two or more sets of sounds (voices) and/or sights (pictures) and/or sensations and/or emotions, generally without conscious awareness.

Attaching/Anchoring (Obsessive/Compulsive): Repetitively playing out one set of sounds (voices) and/or sights (pictures) and/or sensations and/or emotions.

Identification/Sensitization: Increasing responsiveness to sounds (voices) and/or sights (pictures) and/or sensations and/or emotions.

Tolerance/Desensitization (Habituation): Decreasing responsiveness to sounds (voices) and/or sights (pictures) and/or sensations and/or emotions.

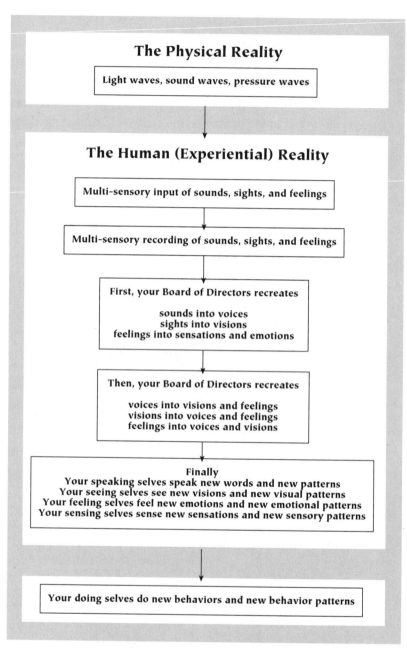

The Physical Reality

Light waves, sound waves, pressure waves

The Human (Experiential) Reality

Multi-sensory input of sounds, sights, and feelings

Multi-sensory recording of sounds, sights, and feelings

First, your Board of Directors recreates

sounds into voices
sights into visions
feelings into sensations and emotions

Then, your Board of Directors recreates

voices into visions and feelings
visions into voices and feelings
feelings into voices and visions

Finally
Your speaking selves speak new words and new patterns
Your seeing selves see new visions and new visual patterns
Your feeling selves feel new emotions and new emotional patterns
Your sensing selves sense new sensations and new sensory patterns

Your doing selves do new behaviors and new behavior patterns

TRANSFORMATIONAL PROCESS OF YOUR BOARD OF DIRECTORS

What is the source of behavior? When you take in data, your Board of Directors recreates what you hear, see, and feel into your past history.

C H A P T E R   F O U R

Stress: The 20th Century Plague

THE DOWNSIDE OF BEING IN TOUCH with your physical feelings is stress. I've talked about stress already, and we'll mention it more as we go along in this book. It is the twentieth century version of the bubonic plague, wiping out people in business left and right.

Business for verbal brainers is mainly a numbers game. Budget and bid out the plant expansion. Get the bodies in motion to finish the project in X number of weeks—bring it in under budget (at whatever cost is necessary in stress to human beings working on the project).

For visual brainers, it's a vision quest. They have this marvelous *sense* of where they want to go and take their people. They tend to be dissatisfied with the here and now; they live, instead, fantasy-like, in the Promised Land of the Vision.

Business for the physical feelers is primarily an athletic event or war! Somewhere between soccer, football, and mud wrestling. It's: "Let's get out there and charge that hill!" Physical feelers frequently experience stress as positive.

For emotional feelers, business is a morality play. This is ultra important to understand, because if emotional feelers decide the boss is unethical or wrong, they will be willing to take down the whole ship to get back at him or her. Their motto is: "I don't care whether you like me or not. What I want is for you to respect me." Until all the players are wearing white hats—or the guys with the black hats have been hamstrung—these types are likely to feel themselves as working under stress.

The positive side of the emotional feelers is what we call charisma. Remember, our working definition of charisma is not walking on water or raising the dead. It's: "If I feel good when I am around you, I will tend to see you as charismatic." In other words, the followers identify the leader as the wellspring of their positive vibes. Or their negative vibes. In either case, stress accompanies their emotional outflow.

The Stress Converter

Hardiness is invaluable. In fact, if a leader doesn't have it, he or she may end up as duck soup. It's the quality we need when storm clouds are flying. It's what lets us turn bad stress into good stress.

Hardy people will know how to shake loose and party even in the midst of chaos and fear and threat. That's real hardiness.

Rainy day...Awful, ain't it? No, it doesn't have to be. Like Gene Kelly we can all dance in the rain.

Hardiness involves a flexibility to use your voices, visions, and feelings to create an inner experience that is positive regardless of what's going on outside in the external universe.

Put in physiological terms, hardiness is the capacity

Stress: The 20th Century Plague

to convert distress into good stress. Physically, hormonally, neuronally, or neuro-transmitter-wise, what's going on in the body is exactly the same with either bad or good stress. It's all adrenaline, cortisone, and caffeine dumps. What the hardy individual does, however, is interpret through his voices and visions the way he sees himself and other people so as to transform their awareness from bad to good.

It's how they talk to themselves. If you tell yourself, "Aw, crud, it's pouring. This rain is ruining everything!" that's about the way you'll feel inside. If you say to yourself, "Cool! A really dramatic, turbulent rainstorm. Don't see this often, may as well enjoy it," how you feel about the day—and about yourself—will be radically different.

And how we talk to ourselves leads directly to how we talk to other people. We even, by our tone and our words, start to shape *their* reactions to us. You want to create some negative vibes around you? Start talking negatives. If you'd like to generate a positive atmosphere, you had better start by being positive in your own conversation with yourself, and then in your outer conversations with others.

Negative stress is far more likely to lead to chronic problems, things that won't go away, such as high blood pressure, ulcers, and death. But this doesn't have anything to do with the mere dumping of the hormones—or of adrenaline. That'll be the same whether the stress is positive *or* negative.

The art of life lies in constant readjustment to our surroundings.

—*Okakura Kakuzo*

The nature of the stress is dependant on how the individual interprets the stressful situation—the typically hardy individual is able to shed stress after the moment has passed. Instead of bottling all the stress up inside and letting it cook and simmer, let go of it and get back to a relaxed state.

Handle Your Stress Like a Cat

Watch an animal, a cat, for instance, that's being chased. Watch the cat, lying quietly on the lawn licking its paws, when a dog comes along. The dog lights out after the cat and the cat has to flee to a rooftop. I mean, that cat had to get into full gear just to get away, but once the cat's on the rooftop, what does it do? It lies down, licks its paws, and stretches out to catch some sun.

The cat was interrupted in the midst of a tranquil moment. Suddenly, the cat was presented with a life-threatening situation. It dumped all the adrenaline it could muster and ran like hell. Now that was good—and necessary. We all need to be able to do that. But after the danger has passed, we also should be like the cat and let go, get back to a normal, relaxed state.

It's when we hold onto the stress—and we're ten times as likely to hold onto *bad stress* as onto *good stress*—that we have a continuing physiological process of dumping hormones and adrenaline. This keeps us in a high state of anger, fear, or tension. It's like running your car

---

No leader, however great a personality he may be, is as important to people as their own intellectual development.

—G.W. Russell

in first-gear when you're out on a 65-mph highway.

The result of this will be everything we don't want: high blood pressure, cardiovascular problems, spastic colon, cancers, strokes, you name it.

Hardy people know how to handle stress. And they are especially good at turning bad stress into good stress, so that they can get through it, let go of it—and then go play golf.

Wearing Yourself Out with Worry

They don't call it "killer stress" for nothing. Our bodies are robust. We can handle tremendous amounts of wear and tear, both physical and psychological. At some point, though, we crack.

Let's say I am a worrier. Worrying is nothing but a state of awareness or consciousness. If I'm a worrier, I have voices in my head arguing with each other all the time: "Should I or shouldn't I do this or that? What's right, what's wrong?" Not only will I worry over my own problems, I'll take on those of my spouse, parents, children, or colleague at the next workstation.

Keeping myself in such a high-pitched state of negative awareness all the time is debilitating. By staying in such a state, I am dumping all my stress hormones into my physical and emotional systems night and day.

This kind of abuse will produce all sorts of functional changes in my body. Tension will tighten my stomach. Peptic acid, hydrochloride, and other juices will ooze out in oversupply and trigger indigestion, heartburn, and perhaps kidney problems. Some people who worry constantly will run their blood pressure up.

Because our bodies are sturdy and resilient by design, these increased tensions and fluids won't make too much difference—for awhile. Especially if I'm taking Maloxx and eating right. Good nutritional habits will tend to counterbalance the excess acid in my gut.

Bit by bit, though, the acids will eat a hole in my stomach lining. And presto! there I am with an ulcer. An ulcer is an extremely worrisome phenomenon; so, of course, now I will worry even more intensely.

As I continue to worry, however, the hole gets bigger. I dump even more acid, and so I get into a downward spiral, plunging further and further into distress, fear, and anguish.

I'll probably try to fight these symptoms with massive doses of drugs, including some which may have harrowing side effects.

Do you see where worrying all the time can lead?

Now what should you do about all this if you are a worrier? (And why not try to do something effective *before* you get that ulcer?)

Finding the Positive Light

To begin with, you need to learn to talk to yourself differently. That may sound like a piece of cake, elementary, but it's not nearly as easy as it sounds.

The weather is not a bad place to start. Try finding something positive to tell yourself about *every* day. Even the dreary, gray, drizzly ones. Even if it's just, "Well, this will sure help me appreciate the sun when it decides to come back."

There was a recent TV commercial in which a teenage girl is saying, "One of the things my dad told me is when you're out sailing, rather than cursing the wind, change your sail."

See, I may not be able to change *you* or the way you

behave that has been grating on me, but I can change my way of perceiving you or evaluating your behavior. If I can do that, I can shut down a lot of my inner negativity and turmoil.

At work, start trying to cast *all* situations in a positive light. Instead of saying, "Terrible things are happening. My boss thinks I'm a jerk. I'm liable to get fired!" how about: "Look what's going on here. It may be part of a universal plan to help me make a healthy adjustment in my life and get into a situation where I can work with really compatible people, so I can feel appreciated and worthwhile." Or you may want to try: "I really like this place where I'm working, except for my problems with my boss. How can I shift my vision and my energy to defuse this conflict?"

Powerful Stress Management

To be a leader you must learn to master your inner self in order to be comfortably uncomfortable in a difficult situation. Transforming bad stress into good stress is the way to become a powerful leader. You are a leader because you lead yourself for better or worse. You also experience stress because life is difficult at times for you. There are many different ways in which you can learn to deal with stress; here's a method that worked for one woman.

> *My Stress-self began to surface after the birth of my second son. My life script was that of all-giving mother and left no part for myself or my husband. The event that triggered change in my life was when my husband knocked my three-year-old son down in a fit*

of rage. I insisted my husband attend a self-awareness workshop; I went, too.

The first step I took was to become aware of some parts of myself that I didn't want to see. Through a meditation process using breath work, I became aware of a great deal of rage. One of the most helpful models was one that made me aware that I was responsible for my own feelings. It was called ARAC—Awareness, Responsibility, Assert, Create.

My method of stress management was to look at myself inside and allow myself to be angry, and later on, allow myself to cry and grieve. I wrote down all the angry words I wanted to say to anybody and everybody in a journal. I also joined a support group, where people let me talk about the stressful things in my life and made me realize I wasn't such a bad person after all. I believe that stress management has a lot to do with accepting human love or divine (self) love.

From the group, I also learned that listening is a wonderful stress management tool. I listen to myself when I meditate and I listen more to other people. I can listen to the "bad feelings" of my husband or sons and still accept them and love them.

When my Stress-self reappears and I get angry or scared, I manage the stress by using a model called "Voices, Visions, and Feelings." I tell myself things I need to hear when I feel stressed. Some examples are: "I love you, it's going to be all right, and you can do it." I see beautiful pictures in my mind—such as a mountain, a river with lots of rocks and whitewater, or a clear mountain lake. I love to see blue sky and quiet woods.

Sometimes I see the face of a person I love. I see this person smiling at me and hear the voice of this person. If someone is verbally attacking me, I remember the other person who loves me. The experience of being loved can be a powerful stress management tool. I can recall this love at any time, even though the person isn't physically with me.

This process of seeing visions and hearing voices is not easy at work because of all the distractions. However, it only takes a second to remember or see something pleasant. For me, the best stress management technique in this model of "Voices, Visions, and Feelings" is to remember the feeling of being loved. Hugging is a great way for me to remind myself that I am loved.

At first, it was scary for me to ask for a hug from people at work, but it turned out that they liked it, too. I am still not a great hugger because my Stress-self interferes a lot and I feel scared. However, I believe the ARAC model has helped me assert and create this hugging and loving side of me.

Another way in which I manage my stress through the "Voices, Visions, and Feelings" model is to listen to music or sing songs. My feelings are activated by music. Peaceful music will calm me; rock and roll will get me *going. At work or home, I sing to myself the type of song I need to hear. "Peace Is Flowing Like a River" is a good song to sing at work when my coworkers are trying to bite my head off. "Take This Job and Shove It" is a great song when I'm angry.*

Whatever technique I use, I maintain the Primary Operational Principle of Leadership: turn bad stress into good stress.

C H A P T E R   F I V E

Leadership Styles: Traditional vs. Participative

IN TODAY'S CORPORATE WORLD, there are, fundamentally, two opposing styles of leadership—traditional and participative. Plus, there are companies either trying to blend the two or caught in the maelstrom of trying to convert from one to the other.

The *traditional style* has been our leadership mode for centuries. It is embodied in one honcho at the top who is supposed to oversee everything; who calls all the shots, cracks the whip, and marshals the troops. This style built empires for Alexander the Great, Julius Caesar, and innumerable French and British kings throughout history. Many traditional leaders have followed Machiavelli's counsel to use cruelty or torture whenever good will or amiability fell short.

It's no different in a corporation. You have some benevolent traditionalists and some tyrants, with shades of everything in between.

What's more, as we have already learned, subordinate leaders will ape the top leader's style. At NationsBank, for example, confronting one another in open, no-nonsense terms is seen as a positive, because Hugh McColl, chairman and CEO, does this himself.

The motto of the traditional leader is: "Command and control." This leadership style is task- and action-oriented. For those of you familiar with the Myers-Briggs psychological testing model, it's very STJ (sensor/thinker/judge). Action, control, structure. Plan everything out, then stick to the plan. All this feeds into generating confrontations among various executors of the plan who may disagree on emphasis, tactics, or expected outcomes. There are many examples of this style in Fortune 500 companies, but General Electric especially is noted for it.

GE's CEO, Jack Welch, has the nickname "Neutron Jack." Do you know what a neutron bomb does? It takes out the people but lets the buildings stand. And Jack Welsh didn't get the nickname for nothing.

Looking back over the political and industrial history of the United States, the traditional style is dominant. People who've made a difference have often been the strong, independent, bright, creative, high-profile types of leaders.

Train 'Em Up Instead of Firing Them

Recently, however, another style has emerged and is making its presence felt—the *participative mode of*

See Chapter 6 for more information about the Myers-Briggs test.

Leadership Styles: Traditional vs. Participative

running a private or public unit. Today perhaps 10–15 percent—at most—of our American companies walk and talk this relatively new, team-oriented, "pull-together," mutually supportive, empowering style.

Frequently, within this style, the leader will not have, or won't bother to cultivate, a high profile. He or she is much more interested in developing leadership capabilities down through the ranks and, thus, building a strong team.

The motto of the participative leader is: "Train 'em up!" The reason for the motto is that there tends to be a high appreciation of human resources and of the human capacity for learning and flexibility within participative leadership structures.

You can really tell the difference in philosophy between traditional and participative organizations by looking at how they go about the pursuit of cost-effectiveness.

In the traditional bailiwicks, cutting costs usually means cutting people. It's enlightening to see that in the traditional scenario, the more people a CEO cuts, the "leaner and meaner" he reshapes his unit to be, the more money the CEO gets paid. That is, the bigger the CEO's salary and bonus become. These types of leaders are having a field day in the current corporate climate—ripping and downsizing like crazy. And they blame it all on the mantra of the day: "We've got to cut costs!"

Meanwhile, in the small but rapidly growing participative group, leaders are merging and acquiring like honeybees scooping up nectar. When BB&T (Branch Bank & Trust, headquartered in Winston-Salem, North Carolina) acquires a thrift or financial institution, it has a no-layoff policy. BB&T tells the people in the newly acquired company right up front: "We are *not* going to lay you off because of the acquisition."

Now if you don't lay them off, what do you do with them? For example, let's say you've already got two auditors at a particular location and all you need is one. What are you going to do with that spare auditor?

Retrain! Take his innate generous capacity for learning and teach him to do something else that the company can use. With the motto, "Train 'em up," the participatives are investing heavily in all manner of training techniques and technology, seminars, short-courses, video courses, and apprenticeships.

What have organizations such as Hewlett-Packard and Ben & Jerry's discovered? In a democratic environment, nine times out of 10 a team of individuals who are moderately intelligent and creative will beat the pants off of a traditional group where you have one bright, creative, aggressive fountainhead presiding over a bunch of lobotomized individuals.

To Kill the Tail, Chop off the Head

Historically, industry's philosophy has been, "Hire bodies," preferably ones that aren't too bright. In highly regulated industries, such as trucking or assembly-line work, it can be a problem when people think too much or get creative with the regulations. You just want them lockstepping and rolling up profits for you.

In the short run, this has worked fairly well. You can run off of the energy of a Henry Ford or an Alfred Sloane or a Hugh McColl or a Bill Gates for quite a while. But what happens if Bill Gates gets hit by a bus? Or if Henry Ford had had a heart attack *before* he got the whole assembly line thing going? Where is the genius and the drive to fill in the gap that the demise or incapacitation of the great traditional leader will leave?

You see, if the fountainhead gets hit by a bus, and that person has not spent enough time, money, and effort training up someone else, the company is in a bad place. The Mafia had a saying in its endeavor to get Bobby Kennedy and the Justice Department investigators off their backs, "To kill the tail, chop off the head."

Now nobody has ever proved that the Mafia had anything to do with the assassinations of either Bobby or Jack Kennedy. But it's clear that Mafia leaders were at least talking about such "solutions" to their dilemma at a meeting in New Orleans in the early '60s.

What do the defensive linemen and linebackers try to do to gain advantage in an NFL game? Sack the quarterback, over and over and over, until he's so bruised or tired or discouraged that he falls apart. That will effectively kill the opposing team's drive to win.

The same thing is true in a traditional corporate environment. If you get rid of the autocrat, another one will replace him. Before that occurs, however, you'll probably see warfare in the ranks and lots of bloodletting and wasteful confusion.

In the participative sector, where they are busy spending time and energy training people to be both management generalists and specialists, you can't sabotage a whole company just by wearing down the chief executive. The CEO can have a stroke or a heart attack or even jump ship, and trained-up team workers will soon cover the gap. The company may be jolted for a short while, but it will mend its own wounds and move ahead.

The Participative Wannabees

In between the autocrats and the participatives, we need to take note of a third group: *the participative wannabees*. Here leaders talk the lingo of participative management, but they walk the old traditional style. That's right, watch your back!

Within the wannabees there are two subgroups. One group has no more intention of turning into a participative than a dog has of turning itself into a cat. They are just using whatever comes down the pike, picking up on all the management fads as they come into vogue. Such management is essentially autocratic and manipulative. Fundamentally, they have no intention of changing their stripes.

In the other subgroup, the CEO and other top people truly want to make the jump from traditional to participative, but they don't have a real clue as to how to go about it. They don't have any idea how to approach such a shift because their entire career has been spent in the traditional domain and they've had a certain measure of success with that style. But now they are reading the business journals and looking over their shoulders at participative competitors and struggling to catch up with what appears to be the more productive style.

I find that the great thing in this world is not so much where we stand, as in what direction we are moving. We must sail sometimes with the wind and sometimes against it—but we must sail, and not drift, nor lie at anchor.

—Oliver Wendell Holmes, Jr.

Can Leaders Change Styles?

The good news about the profession of leadership is that you don't have to change anything inside of you to be a leader. Your values, your beliefs, your feelings, your needs—all these can stay as they are. Not only do you not have to change anything, but from my perspective, nobody has a right to ask you or tell you to change anything inside of you. That's not *their* territory; that's *your* territory.

The bad news about leadership is that you *do* have to change your overt behavior—if you want to be successful. *Feel* however you want, in other words, but *behave* in the way that works for the particular situation you're in. And that way may or may not be congruent with your feelings.

The Intrapersonal Leaderself Development Program

"Intra" means within. And so, to develop as a powerful, participative, and charismatic leader, you must, first, be aware of your self and, second, be aware of others. Teamleadership begins by first focusing within and then focusing outward.

Skillful contemporary leadership requires that the leader be aware of and fluent in at least three languages: verbal brain language, visual brain language, and feeling (mid) brain language. In other words, you must be able to communicate with the following types of people:

■ Those who are bottom line oriented and see business as a numbers game (verbal).

■ Those who are picture and pattern oriented and view business as a vision quest (visual).

73

■ Those who are action oriented and view business as an athletic event (physical feeling).

■ Those who are team oriented and consider business as a morality play (emotional feeling).

Managers are most skillful at the verbal brain language. Next is the visual brain language. Leaders most need to learn and understand emotional feeling brain language.

Positive, creative leadership requires developing the

Positive and Negative Personality Characteristics of Leaders

🖘 *In the intrapersonal leadership process, it is important to be aware of the best and the worst of our selves. Let's look at the best and worst of traditional and participative leaders:*

Traditional (autocratic)	Participative (team-oriented)
One person/party rule	Two or more person/party rule
Motto: Command and Control	Motto: Train 'em up

ADVANTAGES	
Clear thinking, consistent	Adaptable, affectionate
Considerate, conventional	Appreciative, conscientious
Courageous, daring	Cooperative, caring, considerate
Dominant, efficient	Easygoing, emotional, sensitive
Forceful, formal	Fair-minded, forgiving, sincere
Frank, independent	Friendly, gentle, sociable
Industrious, logical	Good-natured, helpful
Methodical, organized	Honest, idealist, open
Outspoken, practical	Tactful, kind, trusting
Precise, rational	Loyal, moderate, understanding
Realistic, reasonable	Patient, pleasant, praising
Reliable, responsible	Progressive, warm, unselfish
Cool, self-confident, self-assured	Reflective, relaxed, versatile
Shrewd, stable	Resourceful, sensitive, warm
Strong, tough	Sociable, understanding

Leadership Styles: Traditional vs. Participative

Leaderself. The Leaderself is that state of awareness that you ideally operate out of when you are in your leadership role. The Leaderself can learn, develop, and grow by developing fluency and skill with the three languages, especially the feeling brain language.

The biggest obstacle you have to powerful, flexible changes is your Stress-self. Your Stress-self is that state of awareness that stops your Leaderself from operating

Competitive, thorough	Spontaneous, sympathetic
Brave, bold	Tactful, tolerant, trusting
Active, adventurous	

DISADVANTAGES

Traditional Moderate	**Participative Moderate**
Aggressive, argumentative	Absentminded, affected
Arrogant, autocratic	Anxious, apathetic, unrealistic
Sarcastic, bossy, assertive	Careless, cautious
Demanding, faultfinding	Complaining, defensive
Hardheaded, hard-hearted	Dependent, disorderly
Impatient, intolerant, ambitious	Fearful, high-strung
Stubborn, tactless	Inhibited, irresponsible
Reckless, rigid, stubborn	Nervous, resentful, worrying
Tense, unemotional	Self-denying, soft-hearted
Unkind, unscrupulous	Temperamental, timid, touchy
Quarrelsome, distant	Passive-aggressive, withdrawn
Unenthusiastic, boring, gloomy	

DISADVANTAGES

Traditional Militants	**Participative Militants**
Psychopathic, homicidal	Meek, submissive
Manic, hateful, evil	Self-punishing, evil
Cold, deceitful	Terrified, obsessive
Hostile, enraged	Compulsive
Stubborn, rejecting	Suicidal, depressive
Vicious, addictive	Masochistic
Cruel, paranoid	Addictive

Positive and Negative Behaviors of Leaders

The team leader employs whichever style (traditional, participative, or a combination of the two) that is appropriate to the follower or situation.

Traditional (autocratic)	Participative (team-oriented)
One person/party rule	Two or more person/party rule
Motto: Command and control	Motto: Train 'em up

ADVANTAGES

Short-term efficiencies	Long-term efficiencies (TQM)
Quick decision making and problem solving because of centralized decision making	Thorough examination of decisions and problems
Empowers the leader	Empowers the followers
Suppresses divisiveness and conflict in the group	Surfaces differences and conflicts in the group
Money and status rewards are primary tools	Praise and encouragement are primary tools
Task-oriented—gets the job done	People-oriented—gets the most out of followers
Clearly defined subdivision in assigning work	Flexibility defined subdivision in assigning work
Strong dependence of subordinates on boss	Strong dependence of subordinates on each other
Rewards external to tasks	Reward in work
Work through "formal organization"	Work through "formal organization"
Hierarchical organization. Greater reliance in individual decision making	Matrix organization. Greater reliance on group decision making
Openly and directly shares strengths and weaknesses of tasks, products, and services	Openly and directly shares strengths and weaknesses of self
Emphasizes *discipline* of self and others	Emphasizes *caring*, consideration, and fairness
Type A	Type B
Structure and form	Feelings and process
Sees productivity in terms of task, product, or service	Sees productivity in terms of people and process

Leadership Styles: Traditional vs. Participative

DISADVANTAGES	
Traditional	**Participative**
Triggers attack/avoidance behavior in followers	Triggers passive behavior in followers
Stifles imagination and creativity	Stifles individual initiative and ambition
Short-sighted decision making and problem solving	Slow and laborious initiative and ambition
"CYA"	"Don't give a damn"
Elevated level of anger, frustration and impatience "leaves bodies strewn in his wake"	Elevated level of fear, guilt, and hurt
Elevated use of denial. Don't see, don't hear, don't feel. Hides/denies perceived weaknesses	Elevated use of rationalization, "ain't if awful," rationalized perceived weaknesses
Paternalistic	Maternalistic
Narrow span of control	Broad span of control
"Lone Ranger" syndrome: "every man for himself"	Bureaucracy "split the difference"
Defers up, controls down, competes laterally	Defers down, controls up, cooperates laterally
Blames others	Blames self
"Mushroom theory of leadership"	Placating
"Shoots the messenger" and doesn't know it	Shoots self and doesn't know it
Adversarial	Chaotic

from a powerful, effective, and sensitive state. Your Stress-self blinds, deafens, and depotentiates your Leaderself. The Stress-self is also the part of you of whom you are *least aware*.

The powerful leader continually works at mastering his or her inner psychological process of being *comfortably uncomfortable* in difficult, demanding, or stressful leadership situations. The skill to transform "bad" stress into "good" stress is an essential tool in the kitbag of the powerful leader.

The Interpersonal Leaderself Development Program

The leadership process is a process of *creating, building, and maintaining relationships* among the leaders' "selves" and the followers' "selves." Leaders will hire people who *fit* their selves. They will hire the *best* of them and the *worst* of them.

By what a leader does or says or doesn't say or do, the leader creates a leadership development "vacuum" that the followers' selves will "grow up" to fill.

From the individual, personal perspective, perceptions tell you about the perceiver, not the perceived. Your perceptions tell you about *your* needs, values, and attitudes, not those of the perceived.

On the other hand, the followers' perceptions tell about the leader's organizational leadership style. The perceptions, attitudes, and feelings of the followers are a function of the conditions created by the leadership. The leader's style is expressed in the responses and behaviors of the followers.

Diversity: The American or Democratic Advantage

The single greatest weakness of the traditional leadership style is its tradition of concentrating power with one person and the resulting homogeneity of the followers.

The leader works in the open, and the boss in covert. The leader leads, and the boss drives.

—Theodore Roosevelt

Leadership Styles: Traditional vs. Participative

The primary teamleadership or democratic advantage is that the wide diversity of thoughts (values and beliefs), feelings (emotional and physical), and actions (internal and external) of the followers creates the greatest possibility of the *highest quality of creative, innovation, original problem-solving, and powerful charismatic leadership.*

Read, Feed & Lead

How do you gain awareness of self and others—the prime ingredient for teamleadership? Use the *Read-Feed-Lead process.* The most important person to Read-Feed-Lead is you. Secondly, you must Read-Feed-Lead your followers. Here's how it works:

■ **Read** the person or situation.

■ **Feed** back to the person your message, purpose, or intention to work with, support, or assist this person *in the language of the person.*

■ **Lead** the person or situation to work with, support, or assist you in accomplishing the task, mission, or goal *in the language of the person.*

Your goal is to Read-Feed-Lead your self into the "best of you," that emotional state of you in which you feel *peaceful, powerful, and focused.*

PART TWO

Leadership
Strategies

C   H   A   P   T   E   R   S   I   X

Grow Your Leaderself

GROWTH WILL OCCUR if you recognize both your strengths and your weaknesses, and work to turn weaknesses into strengths. As a leader, you will not get far by pleading inherent, unchangeable weak spots: "I just fly off the handle occasionally, hell, that's just the way I am." Or: "I keep losing track of things, I've always been somewhat absentminded. What do you expect? Nobody's perfect."

Such rationalizing is unacceptable and counterproductive for anyone seriously interested in improving leadership capacity.

One excellent way to work on your weak spot is to ddliberately seek out relationships, professional or social, with people who have "grown up" parts of the human capacity that you have not. Such people may be prompt where you are tardy, or courageous where you are fearful, or confident where you are full of self-doubt. Working with them or even spending time with them will show you a model for the behavior you are after and put you under pressure to behave more as they do.

These are good things, even though they will cause you some pain.

As an overly laid-back, phlegmatic type, you may feel like shying away from a company where people are energetic in tackling and solving problems, where workers forge ahead. Well, that company may be just what you need to shake off your lethargy.

The contrary is also true. The hard-charging, never-say-die executive who is on the verge of stressing himself into a cardiac episode or a nervous collapse may find that taking a job in a smaller, less-stressful community and learning how to go home at six o'clock is, quite literally, what a doctor might order. What, after all, is the good of becoming a super producer if your family has to bury you when you're forty-six?

Intrapersonal Management

Leadership is essentially an intrapersonal management process. The more you understand about **you,** the more you're going to understand about other people.

One highly practical and reliable way to learn about you is by taking the Myers-Briggs test. Based on the trailblazing psychological work done by Carl Jung, the Myers-Briggs is an accurate, valid, and proven instrument for charting personality.

I recommend this test for anyone bent on developing his or her leadership capacity. Those seriously interested

You cannot be a leader, and ask other people to follow you, unless you know how to follow, too.

—Sam Rayburn

in participative leadership should encourage everybody in their unit to take the test, because then you can really see why people interact, positively or negatively, the way they do. You can then make some allowance for type differences. This will facilitate all your teamwork and also your one-on-one interfaces.

Sometimes the Myers-Briggs strikes people as complex and, thus, intimidating. For that (as well as other) reasons, some people shy away from taking it—or if they take it, they don't treat the results seriously enough. These are mistakes. The Myers-Briggs can be one of your leading allies for getting to the root of conflict, poor communication, and counterproductive behavior going on right under your nose.

How the Myers-Briggs Test Works

Let's break the Myers-Briggs down into bite-size chunks and make it digestible. Maybe then it won't be as intimidating and you'll go ahead and take it and greatly add to whatever insights you've received from this book.

Myers-Briggs delivers a readout on each personality tested that amounts to a combination of four letters. ENTJ, for example, is one possible combination. The letters represent choices of pairs—such as extrovert or introvert (E or I)—for each of four categories. In other words, for each category tested, you are either predominantly one way or the other.

Extrovert or Introvert

The first pair of choices in the Myers-Briggs is: **extrovert** or **introvert (E or I)**.

Extroverts take the energy that is available to them and push it back out into the atmosphere around them. They put energy into interacting with the environment "out there." Introverts take the same energy and let it run around inside their minds and their feelings. A little bit of energy gets put out into the atmosphere, but not much.

Extroverts focus on the world of people and things. They tend to be more talkative and public-oriented than introverts. Frequently, they will say whatever pops into their minds, sometimes almost as a substitute for thinking. If you don't know what an extrovert is thinking, you weren't listening. Extroverts have to experience life in order to understand it. This means they are most comfortable experimenting, trying things out, taking risks if need be. Typically, extroverts are more socially oriented than introverts. If you go to a party with an extrovert, after two or three hours, you'll see that your friend is just "getting started." Go to a party with an introvert and your companion will be ready to leave almost as soon as you get there. They're only staying because you're their ride home.

Introverts focus on the inner world of ideas and concepts. Still waters run deep. In place of talking, introverts *think*. If you don't know what an introvert is thinking, you forgot to ask. Frequently, however, they'll make the mistake of assuming that you already know what they're thinking when, in fact, you don't. To know, you have to ask, draw them out. Introverts also tend to be more territorial than extroverts. They have a clearer sense of "what's mine" and "what's yours" and where the line between the two should be drawn. You don't want to step over that line!

Sensor or Intuitive

The second pair of choices in Myers-Briggs—**sensor** or

intuitive—is a look at how a given individual perceives things and how he or she organizes those perceptions. Myers-Briggs says that we see things predominantly from a sensing perspective or an intuitive perspective. The letter for sensors is "S," for intuitives "N" (not "I").

Sensors trust, use, and rely upon their five senses— smell, sight, hearing, touch, and taste. What you see, in other words, is what you get: whatever is concrete and perceivable through the senses. Such individuals are fond of "sticking to the facts." They like details, statistics, and hard evidence. They tend to be very much "here and now" oriented. They are not, that is, wrapped up in either the past or the future. "What's the problem?" is a favorite question of sensors. And their typical response is, "Let's deal with it right now." Sensors thus value "common sense" and like to work through a problem in a clear-cut, linear A-B-C way.

Intuitives, as the tag implies, are much more prone to rely upon hunches, "gut feelings," creativity, imagination, and "chemistry." They love to call up experiences from the past and compare them to the present, and they're also apt to indulge in "what if we did such and so" scenarios to plot out the future. Intuitives like and often trust abstractions, ideas, concepts, and possibilities.

Watching a sensor and an intuitive work on a problem together is a hoot. The sensor goes through A, B, C, D, and E, while the intuitive says, "Yeah, but what about X

Greatness of soul consists not so much in soaring high and in pressing forward, as in knowing how to adapt and limit oneself.

—Montaigne

or Y?" Sensors prefer tangible, concrete things. Intuitives love to kick back with their eyes closed and conjure up a vision of a project's outcome.

If you go into a sensor's office and say, "I've got an idea but I haven't completely thought it through yet," the sensor is likely to respond, "Well, go back to your place and think some more. When you've got it all down, come back and we'll talk." Whereas an intuitive would say, "Terrific, come on in and I'll help you brainstorm it."

If you go into an intuitive's office and say, "I've got this idea that's really all thought out," the intuitive will be unhappy. You're cutting them out of the shaping process and that's exactly the part they like the most.

Thinker or Feeler

In the third pair of Myers-Briggs categories—**thinker** or **feeler**—the thinker is strongly inclined to rely upon logic, while the feeler puts stock in feelings. The thinker loves to reason things through and leans on intellectual prowess. Whenever confronted with a problem, this type of person will want to sort out "just the facts, Ma'am," and see what, if any, pieces of the jigsaw puzzle are missing and what can be put together.

Feelers look for personal values and feelings. They put great stock in "relationships." They tend to develop, and then draw from, a strongly held set of inner values. These values become their anchor in life and their guide for all decision making.

To a thinker's mind, feelers are "irrational" or "illogical." Thinkers have an easier time cutting through their personal likes and dislikes than feelers do. In fact, if feelers don't like you, they'll take down the whole ship, themselves included, rather than kowtow to somebody they can't respect.

Judges or Perceptives

The final category is: **judges** or **perceptives.** The motto of the judge or J is: "Regulate, control, structure." Judges want order and predictability. They also like to be in control of whatever's going on. If a person is coming out of his J, it does not necessarily mean he's going to be "judgmental." It just means that he'll prefer that things be tied up in nice, neat packages.

Judges also, therefore, tend to be decision oriented. They abhor loose ends, foot-dragging, and sloppiness. Judges sometimes err by rushing to a final decision before one is really warranted.

The perceptive or P tends to be much more process oriented. Perceptives like to allow things to be open and spontaneous, to "go with the flow." They hate being locked into someone else's schedule. They are the gunslingers of the business world. This means they like simply to walk into a situation and deal with things as they come up, without much advance planning. (Judges, of course, are just the opposite.)

Public speakers who are judges are likely to arrive with a detailed outline of what they're going to say—if not the whole speech written out word for word. Perceptives are much better able to speak impromptu, or to veer away from a prepared outline and continue to hold their audience's attention.

In problem-solving groups, judges frequently suffer from premature closure, while perceptives are good at protracting discussion so that closure is kept at bay.

Management Styles

Myers-Briggs identifies four management styles:

■ The Visionary Manager

■ The Troubleshooter

■ The Traditional or Judicial Manager

■ The Catalyst

The Visionary Manager

These are the ENTJs (extrovert/intuitive/thinker/judge), INTJs (introvert/intuitive/thinker/judge), INTPs (introvert/intuitive/thinker/perceptive), and the ENTPs (extrovert/intuitive/thinker/perceptive). Of the four, the ENTJs are the natural visionary leaders. The others have to work harder in their leadership. Nonetheless, the best leader will be whoever is most responsive and flexible in responding to challenges that arise. And really, that can be just as much an INTJ, an INTP, or an ENTP.

All four types have certain problems, but each also has certain strengths.

There are more visionary leaders in senior management ranks than any other type. They're the ones who are good at doing strategic planning for the long haul as well as developing an overarching vision of an organization, including its personnel and its values.

Visionary Manager

ENTJ=extrovert/intuitive/thinker/judge

INTJ=introvert/intuitive/thinker/judge

INTP=introvert/intuitive/thinker/perceptive

ENTP=extrovert/intuitive/thinker/perceptive

The Troubleshooter

ESTP=extrovert/sensor/thinker/perceptive

ESFP=extrovert/sensor/feeler/perceptive

ISFP=introvert/sensor/feeler/perceptive

ISTP=introvert/sensor/thinker/perceptive

The Troubleshooter

Excellent at negotiations, this type often makes a persuasive and decisive executive. The troubleshooter's motto is: "Lead, follow, or get out of the way!" Grouped into this category are the ESTPs (extrovert/sensor/thinker/perceptive), ESFPs (extrovert/sensor/feeler/perceptive), ISFPs (introvert/sensor/feeler/perceptive), and the ISTPs (introvert/sensor/thinker/perceptive). All sensors have a strong orientation toward action—making something happen. However, the way these sensors behave is influenced by the P element. That's why they're called "troubleshooters." They are fabulous at diving into a situation and working with all elements until a compromise or a solution of some kind is hammered out.

The Traditional or Judicial Manager

Here we find the ESTJs (extrovert/sensor/thinker/judge), ISFJs (introvert/sensor/feeler/judge), ISTJs (introvert/sensor/thinker/judge), and ESFJs (extrovert/sensor/feeler/judge). Up until recently, this type reigned unchallenged in the business world. With recent emphasis on team-building and visioning, other types are starting to move up and displace some of the traditionals. The two key elements here are the S, or sensor inclination, and the J, or structuring bent.

At times the traditionals get a bit lost in structure and do not demonstrate the flexibility needed to change horses in midstream when circumstances dictate that they should. But they are good regulators, good at going in there and getting the job done in an organized, detail-conscious way.

The Catalyst

In this group, we find ENFJs (extrovert/intuitive/feeler/judge), INFJs (introvert/intuitive/feeler/judge), ENFPs (extrovert/intuitive/feeler/perceptive), and INFPs (introvert/intuitive/feeler/perceptive). The N or intuitive element is essential to this group. These types are creative, innovative, and imaginative. But the N element is linked with the feeling element rather than with the thinking element. What that means is that the catalysts are equipped to provide the primary vision of an organization. That vision will be more than bricks and mortar. It'll include systems and people.

Catalysts can achieve a picture of how everything ought to, ideally, fit together and work together. They will want people to develop flexible and cooperative patterns and interact in a caring fashion. This is in counterpoint to the visionary manager, whose vision of an organization

The Traditional or Judicial Manager

ESTJ=extrovert/sensor/thinker/judge

ESFJ=extrovert/sensor/feeler/judge

ISFJ=introvert/sensor/feeler/judge

ISTJ=introvert/sensor/thinker/judge

The Catalyst

ENFJ=extrovert/intuitive/feeler/judge

ENFP=extrovert/intuitive/feeler/perceptive

INFJ=introvert/intuitive/feeler/judge

INFP=introvert/intuitive/feeler/perceptive

five years down the road is a 43 percent return on an investment compounded semiannually. Many heads of organizations today are the latter kind of visionary: You go into their office and ask, "What's your vision?" and they whip out the chart with graphs of sales or production figures. Catalysts are different. Ask them their vision and they'll talk about improved communications and how to organize work so that people derive more enjoyment from it.

One thing we're seeing more of in business today is women—and many of them are moving up in management. A lot of these women tend to be INFPs, and they find themselves trying to swim in what is predominantly an ESTJ environment. Everything is precisely opposite to the way they are naturally inclined to think, feel, and behave.

With proper facilitation, however—which might involve outside consultants trained in psychological testing and in behavior and modification—hard-driving male ESTJs actually can learn quite a lot from the female INFPs and begin to adapt, and the female INFPs can learn to modify their internalized, slower-paced ways of acting so that they become more congruent with a growing for-profit organization.

Why the Myers-Briggs Test Scores Are Important

The Myers-Briggs test scores are important because leadership depends heavily upon your capacity to manage relationships. That means you must understand what other people's beliefs and values are, also what their own peculiar brand of craziness is all about. You have to manage right through their acts, their games, the whole nine yards.

Understanding how the Myers-Briggs pinpoints people's personality and, hence, work styles lets you start diagnosing bosses, peers, and subordinates to figure out where they're coming from and how their tapes will play out in the work environment.

All of this is important if a team is to function well and draw from the strengths of all its component members.

Without exception, all of us tend strongly to come out of the essential "rightness" of our beliefs. We thus incline to value in others what we value in ourselves. So if we see ourselves as decision makers and achievers, fast-trackers, movers and shakers—real get-it-done types—we're going to have trouble appreciating people who are a bit slower, who like to reflect and second-guess things. Judges, you can imagine, tend to be real decisive. Perceptors appear to judges as wishy-washy and indecisive. But perceptors look at shades of gray that judges cannot seem to see, and this can be of genuine help to a corporation concerned about making the right choices.

Thinkers tend to discount feelers as being soft, wimpy, and giving away the store. Why, the thinker will say, can't that person be logical, rational, and businesslike?

Sensors are inclined to discount intuitives as being

bubble-headed space cadets—just out there in the ozone getting brain damage from breathing in all of those blue-sky hypotheses.

The Myers-Briggs is a how-you-think, how-you-look-at-the-world kind of instrument. So take a look at how *you* think compared to how *they* think. Look for the disparities. Then see if the problems or conflicts in your relationships with these people stem from ways that you view the world differently and how you process your self-awareness differently (arrive at different conclusions or project the future differently).

Do you want some hard truth? The hard truth is that if you are an STJ, you actually *need* the influence of an NFP. You need somebody who can help you find a sense of long-term direction, somebody who can tell you how to persuade people to buy into the logical decisions you may make as a thinker, because you won't tend to know how to do that, and you need the feelers to show you options that you probably will miss as you come out of your judging instinct.

There is nothing "wrong" with any of the sixteen configurations of letters possible in the Myers-Briggs matrix. Nobody really is any "better" than anybody else. Better at certain things, yes; better in an overall sense, no. It's mainly a matter of becoming aware of what your predispositions or biases are in terms of viewing the world and where those are likely to lead you in your decision making.

Always do right; this will gratify some people and astonish the rest.

—Mark Twain

And after you understand your own wiring, you'll be in much better shape to "read" other people's ways of being and of looking at things.

C H A P T E R   S E V E N

Centering Yourself

THERE ARE TWO TYPES OF CENTERING. The first one is a peaceful centering in your comfort zone. The second type I call "power centering" or "warrior centering."

Peaceful centering consists of learning to stay focused, calm, and relaxed and to respond to situations out of an accepting and loving frame of mind.

Peaceful Centering: One Method

There is some similarity here with the Oriental ways of peaceful meditation—Hindu, Buddhist, Zen.

One model for Peaceful Way centering is that of crafting pottery. To throw a pot properly, you've got to have a certain posture, a certain feel. Very squared off shoulders. You have to hold your pot centered in relation to the wheel. While you are throwing the clay on the wheel, you have to stay "centered," otherwise the clay will fall off to one side or the other. If your body is centered over the wheel, you will experience a kind of mental and emotional centering, too. This centering is translated into the artifact that your hands are molding. Out of this, you will get a symmetrical pot. Balanced, harmonious, aesthetically pleasing.

In contrast, power centering is expanding the comfort zone by hitting the wall. Getting out of the small box and into the big box. Getting into life and death and the dance of the Hindu gods.

It's only in the big box that you get to be like Gandhi, Christ, Martin Luther King, or any other great figure who walks straight into the face of hate and rage with love.

Are great people simply born that way? Was Martin Luther King his great self from the very beginning? Right from the crib? Gandhi, too? I think that stereotype is false. We all have the latent capacity to become Gandhi or Martin Luther King.

There's a progression from awareness of self, to awareness of our potential, to realization of self and potential. But in order to grow in the powerful way, you have to be willing to experience uncomfortable, negative stuff—such as having other people ridicule you or experiencing terrible memories of a repressive childhood.

Power Centering

Power centering prepares you for war. It's the difference between meditation and the martial arts. Whether you're dodging bombs in Bosnia Hertzegovina, living on the south side of Chicago, or flying in the face of a consensus on a board of directors, you'll probably need some power, or warrior, centering.

In leadership, you need to master both the peaceful path and the powerful path. You must learn how to move from one path to the other, as appropriate. If you're dealing with moderates and minnows in an office or political environment, you want to come out of your peaceful way. Why terrorize people who basically are flexible and accommodating? On the other hand, if you're in a war zone, either in fact or metaphorically, you'll need to use power tactics to get people to follow you. Sharks don't follow minnows; they eat them alive. With sharks, you have to be the best of the sharks, and show them that your teeth are bigger and sharper than theirs. (See Multiple Ways on Page 102.)

Breathing Your Way to Power

In order to grow in the Powerful Way, as I've said, you must be willing to experience uncomfortable, negative stuff. Really terrible stuff, sometimes. Sharp criticism, other people's anger, rejection. Feedback that tells you other people think you're doing a poor job.

Learning to do *power breathing* is a big help in growing up to the Powerful Way potential we all have. In power breathing, you pull in oxygen and push out carbon dioxide. You flood the physical feeling part of the brain, mainly the brain stem, the cerebellum, and the reticular activating system, which control much of the automatic sensory physiological functions. Power breathing affects the heart rate, breathing, and digestive system. Then you deluge the systems that channel your emotions.

When you flood your physical and emotional feeling apparatuses, you start to feel things very intensely. You're up against a kind of wall. There's tension in your back and throat. If you continue with the power breathing, even though it feels as if you're going to burst, you'll flood your cerebral parts—the two hemispheres of the brain and the middle brain as well. The verbal brain, voices; the visual brain, visions; the midbrain, feelings.

You probably will enter into a lucid dream state, or some other altered state of consciousness.

Now all your feelings are flooding into the area where

you process your raw sensory awareness into voices and visions. These feelings are welling up, and, experientially, in your heightened awareness, you are hearing voices and seeing visions. Psychologically, you are flying. Just as you might when you are fasting or on a "runner's high."

Such experiences are akin to the mystical, to great spiritual moments. The moments may be heavenly, shot through with a Christ-consciousness or some other divine transcendence. Or they may be hellish, having a nightmarish dimension such as marching lockstep behind Hitler or Stalin.

You may feel rage; you may feel grief; you may feel intense joy. But as you hit the wall and break through, you will experience an expansion of your comfort zone into your power zone. You will move into an area where you will feel empowered to handle the negative, the uncomfortable, and the hopeless. And all of those situations are ones you need to be able to cope with well if you aspire to heavy-duty leadership responsibility. (See the Comfort Zone and Power Zone chart on Page 50.)

Are You Using Peace or Power?

You know by your own inner experience whether you are using peace technology or power technology. If you end up feeling more comfortable and relaxed, it's the peaceful way. If at first you feel uncomfortable and then more powerful, it is the powerful way.

So when you use power training, the key is to use it intentionally, consciously, and in a way that will take you and your follower through it. The powerful way is emotionally intense; it bypasses the verbal brain and the visual brain. It is all feeling, all gut and heart.

When do you use peaceful techniques and when do

you use power techniques? Look at the chart on page 103.

In this chart, positive feelings fall on the scale from 0 to 10. Feeling positive from 0 to 5 is what I call the peaceful way. You feel secure, comfortable, and confident. These are the kind of feelings you get when you are around someone you see as charismatic.

Negative feelings such as sadness, hurt, loneliness, grief, depression, fear, and anger fall on the scale from 0 to -10. There are techniques you can use to climb from the negative side of the scale to the positive.

Let's say you need to climb from a -5 to a +5. This is a slight climb, what you might need to cope with the normal stresses of a normal day. Three peaceful techniques that work well to combat the wear and tear of everyday life are self-talk, self-seeing, and peaceful breathing.

The next time you're stressed out and scraping the -5 on the feelings scale: Go home and take time to do some peaceful meditation—perform some gentle breathing, maybe visualize being at the beach or the mountains, maybe say the rosary or pray.

Whenever you see someone that you perceive as nurturing and caring, sweet and nice, that's charisma at the peaceful way level from 0 to 5. Use the peaceful techniques described above, if you're at a -5 or above, and you can move up the scale.

Peaceful way techniques include prayer, meditation, systematic desensitization (which brings up the negative situation bit by bit, piece by piece, gradually over time). Such techniques will not work for anything above 5. For example, attempting to use peaceful way techniques for a -5 to -10 simply doesn't work. It's like telling a junkie to "just say no" or trying to put out a forest fire

The Multiple Ways

🍃*A good leader uses multiple techniques and strategies depending on the follower. When you as a leader are performing at the Master Level, you are capable of walking both paths—the Peaceful and the Powerful Way.*

The Peaceful Way	The Powerful Way
Motto: A step at a time, day at a time.	Motto: What doesn't kill me makes a me stronger.
1. The Parasympathetic Nervous System	1. Sympathetic Nervous System
2. Accepting & Tenderly	2. Focused & Passionate
3. Step by Step	3. Sink or Swim
4. Gently & Slowly	4. Intensely & Forcefully
5. High MAO	5. Low MAO
6. Yin Way	6. Yang Way
7. Gradually & Progressively	7. Explosively & Powerfully
8. Buddha/Gandhi/King/Christ like	8. Muhammad like, Patton, Jack Welch
9. Romantic	9. Erotic

Peaceful Strategies	Powerful Strategies
1. Traditional feminine/ maternalistic strategies	1. Traditional masculine/ paternalistic strategies
2. New Testament ethics	2. Old Testament ethics
3. Speak from your own experience/heart	3. Guerilla tactics
4. Take responsibility	4. Use Machiavellian approach
5. Use diplomatic approach	5. Use power & confrontation
6. Use praise & personal acknowledgment	

Peace Techniques	Power Techniques
1. Prayer	1. Power anchoring
2. Meditation	2. Power sensing
3. Systematic Desensitization	3. Power dialoguing
4. Focusing	4. Power breathing
5. Peace breathing	5. Sweat Lodge
6. Peace dialoguing	6. Fire walking
7. Peace brainstorming	7. Power moving: repelling, white water, high ropes, etc.
8. Golf	8. War (martial arts)
9. Tennis	9. Power Brainstorming

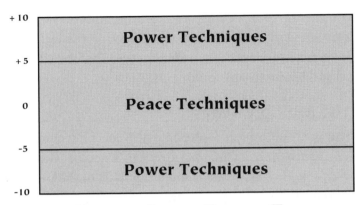

DIFFERENT SITUATIONS CALL FOR DIFFERENT TECHNIQUES

When a small change in state of mind is called for, peace techniques such as prayer, meditation, or peaceful breathing often suffice. However, in more drastic situations, power techniques may be appropriate.

with a garden hose. For these people the powerful way is the only way.

The ground rules for the powerful way are: don't hurt yourself or anyone else. Powerful way techniques often involve intense, powerful, physical movement. Anger just comes up and flies over you. Jogging, running, punching bags, and screaming in the car are all quality ways to displace anger. In the powerful way, you allow the person to have the bad feeling but you try to organize the way the person experiences it and expresses it so the person receives some benefit from it. Then it becomes a learning experience.

As a leader, you must handle people operating anywhere from -10 to +10. You must learn what techniques to use and when. You must know when to persuade in a nice, warm, friendly, diplomatic way and when to get into someone's face. You must master both paths.

Leadership is not a function of the head. It is a function of the heart. It is a function of being in touch with your heart, your feelings, and working with that energy. You can work with the leadership process through both peaceful and powerful way techniques. In fact, the successful leader learns multiple ways.

The Multiple Ways

The peaceful way at a physiological level develops and matures the *parasympathetic nervous system*. The parasympathetic nervous system is that part of the nervous system that relaxes you, producing feelings of tranquillity, calmness, and relaxation. The parasympathetic nervous system slows down your heart rate and lowers your blood pressure. People who prefer the peaceful way tend to have a high level of an enzyme called *monoamine oxidase*. In the East, it's considered the yin way. From a psychological training perspective, it means working with people in an accepting, tender, gentle, and slow manner. Historically, these have been seen as traditionally feminine or materialistic strategies, such as the quiet nurturing of the mother. It is also similar to what I call New Testament ethics, which means that if you are wronged you respond with love, not anger or hate. Take responsibility for your own actions, and in a business environment there is a strong use of praise and acknowledgment of other people and their past accomplishments. Masters of the peaceful way are individuals such as Buddha, Gandhi, Martin Luther King, and Jesus Christ.

Peaceful way techniques include prayer, meditation, systematic desensitization, focusing in a quiet way on different issues or concerns, full, deep, slow breathing, and golf. (Although I've had a few people tell me the way they play golf, it's definitely *not* the peaceful way!) It also includes what I call peace dialoguing, which is dialoguing in a peaceful, diplomatic way, and peace brainstorming, which is reflecting within oneself about issues and concerns.

The motto of the powerful way is what doesn't kill me makes me stronger. Or as we say in North Carolina, rough weather makes good timber. People who wish to walk the powerful way, from a physiological perspective, are attempting to mature and empower the sympathetic nervous system. The *sympathetic nervous system* is the part of the nervous system that gears you up, energizes you, and creates an inner state in which you can act in an intense, forceful, and passionate manner. Physiologically, people who prefer the powerful way as a training methodology tend to have low levels of monoamine oxidase.

If one had a fear of heights, the peaceful way would say go to the second floor, look out the window, remain there until your heart has slowed down and you are comfortable, then go to the third floor and do the same, and then the fourth. Practitioners of the powerful way would immediately go to the rooftop, look over the edge and remain there until they become comfortable with being that high up. In the East, it's called the yang way. It uses traditionally masculine or paternalistic strategies, and Old Testaments ethics. Old Testaments ethics are an eye for an eye, and a tooth for a tooth. If you take out one of mine, I take out one of yours. In a business context, it would mean an equal exchange of value. It is by far the most common path taken by leaders, whether these are business leaders, cultural leaders, or religious leaders. At its best, you have people like Muhammad, George Patton, and Jack Welch. At its worst, you have people like Machiavelli, and Adolf Hitler.

Power techniques include the martial arts and intense athletic activities and sports such as football and hockey. It also includes such techniques as power anchoring, which combines power breathing with internal dialoguing and visioning, to move one into the best of oneself (one's Leaderself) in a powerful, focused and intense manner. Power brainstorming involves first anchoring oneself in one's best qualities and characteristics, and from that perspective bringing up issues and problems and exploring them in a deep, moving and powerful way. Power dialoguing involves engaging others in a dialogue in which one states one's position clearly, passionately, and forcefully. Other examples of power techniques are sweat lodges as practiced by Scandinavians and Native Americans and fire walking.

CHAPTER EIGHT

Ask For Feedback

FOR YOUR LEADERSHIP TO BE EFFECTIVE, you need something that may scare the hell out of you: feedback. Especially negative feedback. You need to know why people hate your guts or think your ideas are looney or believe you're really out for their scalp.

This may not be so easy to arrange. Many employees have been socialized to cover up their anger, to play up to management outwardly (even while stabbing management in the back in conversations among themselves). One reason the bad news doesn't get through is that too many management types have cultivated the bad habit of shooting the messenger. This harks back to medieval days when certain kings would have the bringer of bad news beheaded or riddled with arrows rather than realize that the bad news was exactly the data they needed to have. Obviously, if people think they are going to get shouted down or demoted or fired for bringing you bad news, they will temper the news so it doesn't sound too bad.

One reason so many leaders are leading in the dark is that they don't solicit the really bad news from their followers. Or if they do coax out the bad news from some nervous underling, they don't know how to listen to and use it.

To fix something that's broken, you have to know where to tap. That's why it's important to be able to get the complete lowdown on why systems are running amok or why there is mutiny in the ranks.

I like to use the metaphor of a sea captain who's steering a ship and detects a problem in the steerage column. The captain first asks the ship's engineer to fix the problem, but after a half hour of tinkering, the man comes up with nothing. So the captain sends a helicopter to fetch a high-quality maritime engineer to fix the problem. The quality type comes onto the ship, picks up a hammer, taps at the base of the column—and presto! the steering is completely restored. Then the engineer presents the captain with a bill for $1,000 for two minutes of work. The captain, though pleased with the results, is shocked by the bill, and sends it back with the message: "Please itemize." The bill comes back immediately with the notation: "Tapping hammer, fifty cents. Knowing *where* to tap hammer, $999.50."

As a leader, you must know not only how to wield a hammer but just where to tap. That is to say, you must know exactly what to say or what to do so that your exercise of authority is in line with the values you are trying to project.

Otherwise, you will be perceived as hypocritical, and

We must always change, renew, rejuvenate ourselves; otherwise we harden.

—Goethe

subtly or not so subtly, people will drag their heels in carrying out what you ask, or order, them to do.

Thus, the most powerful tool you can have as a leader is feedback. Ideally, feedback will tell you what's working and what isn't, and how much of the problem resides with *you*. If you can get your people to trust you enough, they will feel free to convey their utterly honest impressions. These should include ways in which you yourself are, from their perspective, off base in your demands, expectations, or style of communicating.

Types of Feedback

One kind of feedback is what I call *management feedback*. This is verbal-brain data about error rate, quality control, and profitability.

A second kind of feedback is *pure leadership feedback*. This kind will tell you just how well, or poorly, you are leading people. Many executives don't care much for this kind of feedback because it targets their personality. It hits them where they live, and they like to put this area off bounds.

While followers often have to crash through many barriers in order to deliver pure leadership feedback, their superiors have to take down just as many obstacles in order to receive it.

To avoid receiving negative feedback, many leaders prefer to operate in a vacuum. That is to say, rather than dig for the root causes of why things are screwed up (especially when they have reason to fear that *their own leadership style* may be the root cause), such leaders take to *guessing* about causes. So they guess and many times they guess wrong. Nonetheless, they will proceed to operate out of their wrong hunch and either screw things up more or waste so much time that the problem just gets worse through inattention.

A number of years ago when I was consulting in a top ten bank, there was a member of the executive operating committee (the team that leads the entire bank) who was going into the committee's meeting with either false information or with huge gaps in his awareness of what was going on in his area and in the bank in general.

I was brought in to conduct a leadership climate study on him and his group. As I did my interviews, I discovered he had a reputation for "shooting the messenger." That is, whenever someone came to him with critical feedback, he would explode at them. This behavior reportedly even occurred in meetings. During the interviews, three people said that the manager had become so angry during a meeting that he took off his shoe and threw it.

Now, I knew this individual even before I went in to do the climate study, and I knew he was not unusually angry or hostile, so I was perplexed as to how he got his reputation. It turns out that the belief/perception that he threw his shoe was started by a disgruntled employee that had been fired. Before the employee left the premises, he planted the rumor.

The effect, predictably enough, was that if the manager showed even a minor degree of irritation, his employees would amplify it in their minds. Before long, the manager's staff was withholding any information that they thought might make him angry.

This illustrates that followers are not necessarily guided in their behavior by the facts, but by their perception of the facts. From a human systems perspective, it doesn't much matter what actually happened, what matters is what is perceived to have happened. It doesn't much matter whether Bill Clinton had affairs or not, the vast majority of his followers believe he did, therefore in their internal psychological reality, he did. It doesn't much matter whether Richard Nixon knew about the Watergate break-ins, the truth is from the perceptions of many of his followers, he did do it.

Though it will be painful for a leader to take in negative feedback about his or her own personality or leadership style, in the end this knowledge will constitute a huge time saver and will quite likely point the way toward effective solutions to problems at hand.

C H A P T E R   N I N E

How To Follow The Followers

ONE OF MY MORE PROVOCATIVE DEFINITIONS of leadership is this: Leadership is knowing how to follow the followers.

Plenty of managers and also pseudo-leaders think that when something happens in their bailiwick that gets results, *they* caused it to happen. They gave an order and other people responded to their authority and did the work and good results followed, for which they, the leaders, usually are all too willing to take credit.

The truth is that there are two parties involved in the interaction we call leadership—the leader and the follower—and they are *both* the cause of results (good or bad).

Leaders cannot cause followers to act in a certain way; they can only provide the conditions within which the followers' motivation for action will be in harmony with the leader's desire.

You never have unmotivated followers. They are always motivated—to pursue what they judge to be in their best interest. To lead, you must identify your followers' highest interests, and then create conditions that dovetail with those interests.

Suppose in a woodworking factory, the followers' highest interests are sufficient breaks and a pleasant work environment. You are not going to match up well if you get rigid with them about their breaks or if you refuse to bring in adequate natural light or if you leave the walls painted a drab gray. They will be happy to follow you once you demonstrate that you are not paranoid about their taking an extra minute or two on break and that you are willing to redo the work environment to suit them.

Always ask yourself the question: What are my followers after? What will it take for them to be willing to carry out what I want them to do? Remember, the followers are always saying within themselves, "I will follow you if what you are asking of me is what meets my needs." Otherwise, you will get a semblance of following—it will be fragile and may, at any moment, collapse into work slowdowns, sloppiness, or resentment of your authority.

So take a look at your followers and ask yourself how they put the world together. Be aware enough, sensitive enough, and open enough to let them spell out their agenda for you.

Reflections of Leadership

🙠 *The perceptions, attitudes, and feelings of the followers are a function of the conditions—both physical and psychological—that are created by the leadership. The leader's style is expressed in the responses, perceptions, and behaviors of the followers.*

Next, adapt yourself so you become able to speak their language. If you can echo their sentiments and hopes, in words and phrases that your people themselves might use, you'll find you'll achieve some powerful resonance with them.

The general principle is you take whatever the environment offers you—that is, whatever the followers provide—and figure out how to use it to further your own purposes and goals. Good leaders don't start with their own needs; they look to what the followers need and then try to match those needs with the situational needs for X-level of production or service.

Different Strokes for Different Folks

Different types of followers will require different handling.

If you've got a Korean War Navy type who just wants to take orders, salute, and do the job, don't bother sitting him down and explaining all the why's and wherefore's. You'll just make him fidgety or you might even lose his respect. Simply hand down the marching orders. On the other hand, if you've got the kind of worker who spent her childhood with chemistry sets and telescopes, tell her as much as you can about process. The more of her questions you answer, the happier she's going to be.

Some of your people may enjoy having you check on them every day. They're the "please-look-over-my-shoulder" types. Others will find constant checking to be irritating and mistrustful; for them, your popping in all the time is insulting. Learn to read your followers and respond to their different ways of following. Believe me, you'll get *much* more out of them!

Does this sound hypocritical? To talk to Dan in one way and to Chad in another? Isn't that being a phony and just trying to "play up" to each of them and manipulate them into doing what you want?

This brings us to what may constitute a shocking revelation to many of you: *Leadership is not about "being yourself."* It is about playing a role, like an actor.

You're on stage in the executive suite. Out there in the office banks and the workstations sit your audience. And to get their applause you have to match up to their expectations of what they want in a leader. Since those expectations will vary from person to person, you will find that, to be effective, you'll have to alter your behavior as you address different elements in your "public."

Seasoned politicians, of course, know this well and make such adaptations all the time. Then the press may catch them in an "inconsistency" and accuse them of *double-talk.* Sometimes they *are* guilty of double-talk, but in other instances they are just putting one emphasis on an issue before one group and looking at another side of the same issue with another group.

Notice that what your followers say is the source or the cause of their positive and negative feelings and actions. What do they claim to be at the root of their reasons for success or for failure? Then see how you can use their responses to promote better outcomes for both them and the company.

When I was doing drug counseling, people would come into my office and blame their problems on pushers or friends or parents or teachers—anybody but themselves. For me, the drugs were secondary. The real issue was hearing what they were saying and then getting them to take responsibility for their behavior—and for changing it.

In leadership/followership terms, some folks will "blame up" (the boss), others will "blame across" (their colleagues), and still others will "blame down" (their subordinates). "The reason we're not doing well as a team is our boss is a jerk," or "If only it weren't for such-and-so having to work with us, we'd get the job done right," or "My people are just plain unmotivated; I can't get 'em to go to the bathroom without showing them the way."

Management will blame the union and the union will state categorically that 100 percent of the problem lies with management.

Weapons for Your Change Battles

After you believe you've really *heard* what is being said, go to work with whatever weapons for change you've got in your arsenal. Some of the most powerful weapons are metaphors, story telling, embedded commands and suggestions, and pattern displacement.

Metaphor

In writing this book I am giving you a metaphor. I'm telling you, "Be aware of your Leaderself, and be aware of your Stress-self." Leaderself is a metaphor, just like the rebellious child and critical parent used in the transactional analysis models or psychologist John Bradshaw's model of "the child within."

A metaphor is just a picture. It's a map that you work with. But it has a powerful reality all its own. Once people buy into the metaphor, they will assign to it enough power to spur dramatic change in their lives.

Story Telling

Fables, parables, and other forms of story telling often constitute a metaphor and are quite frequently the most effective ways for getting people to improve their thoughts and their behavior. Moses and the Promised Land, Ponce de Leon and the search for the fountain of youth, Sleeping Beauty finding her prince, the story of a pilgrim seeking enlightenment on a trek to a distant land, an ambitious Horatio Alger climbing the ladder to success. All stories, all metaphors. It doesn't matter whether your story is "true" or not in literal terms. Make the darn thing up! If your story has psychological impact or metaphorical accuracy, it will advance your purposes.

In your interactions with followers, you need the skill to tell them what you want them to do in such a way that they will do it. Often, the best way to handle this is to convey your achievement goals for them *indirectly,* such as through metaphor or through telling a story. The greater the likelihood of resistance to your statement of goals, by the way, the better will be your chances of success if you use metaphor or narrative.

For example, "John, I once had a friend who had a drinking problem not too different from yours. This guy solved his problem by..." Or, "Greta, anger can be a useful emotion sometimes, as long as we control how and when we use it. I remember a neighbor lady on our block who took charge of her anger by..."

You might have to resort to figures or situations in popular entertainment. Although what goes on in television shows and in movies is not real (a fact some people have a difficult time understanding), it does have, however, a psychological or a metaphorical reality. So you really can talk about an old John Wayne movie or Clint Eastwood or Sly Stallone as Rambo or whatever when making a point, and most of the time, people will buy right into it.

Embedded Commands and Suggestions

Another technique is what I call the "embedded command." You have a suggestion or a command that you want to communicate, but you know instinctively that if you convey it directly, you're going to meet with resistance. So you refer to a previous but similar situation in which this tack worked or you say something like, "I'm sure in my bones that if we'd only go at this problem in such-and-such a way, we'd work it through." Or talk about another company that employed the approach you want and tell how successful they were with it. Doll it up as much as you want, but somewhere embedded in your example or your story you're putting across a command or suggestion.

Replace Denial with "Pattern Prescription"

A fairly typical approach to "helping" other people with problems is to indulge in denial, to pretend the problem doesn't exist—or at least that it's not half as bad as they think it is. Let's say a boss is dealing with a subordinate who is the obsessive/compulsive type and is anguishing over her last less-than-perfect progress report. If the boss says, "Don't worry about it, Kathy," Kathy'll probably double or triple the time and energy she'll put into worrying about her progress report. And worry about it forever.

Leaders who have tried this technique of downplaying or wishing away others' problems can do much better with a technique I refer to as "pattern prescription."

A leader using pattern prescription might say: "Kathy, worrying about problems is a human thing to do. It's just that it's not always productive to do our worrying on company time. What I'd like you to do is schedule your-self a block of time every night to do your worrying, let's say 7 to 7:30 p.m. Then, if you find yourself anguishing over something during the day, tell yourself, 'I'm going to tackle that problem tonight at 7,' and then just get on with your tasks." Believe it or not, this works.

Once a woman came to me and said she was caught up in uncontrollable sobbing. She cried at home, at work, all the time. Her crying had become a problem, not only for herself but also for people around her.

"I went to a psychiatrist and he wanted to give me drugs," she said, "but I didn't want to take them. How-ever, I also don't want to go on crying like this."

"Crying is useful and powerful, " I told her. "It can be a most helpful experience. Crying means that you're in pain, and there's probably a lot for you to learn from that. So what I would like you to do is to plan to cry for about 20 minutes every evening."

When you organize and give people permission for the venting of bad feelings, it's like prescribing a placebo. If people give themselves enough concerted time in which to feel bad, they'll get it out and then they'll feel better."

The other thing, of course, is venting an emotion on a regular schedule gets old. You wear it out. You're sati-ated with it. When it becomes boring enough, you stop.

C H A P T E R   T E N

Try Personality Mentoring

BABIES AND CHILDREN DO observational and associational experiential learning all the time. Children whose parents prize good diction and speech habits usually will follow suit. So will children whose parents are into hard work—or music or sports. How can you use personality mentoring to develop your Leaderself?

It can happen with a boss, a colleague, or even somebody that works for you—anyone who appears to be strong where you have identified yourself as weak. Your mentor can be someone of the opposite sex or someone significantly older or even younger than you.

If you tend to be serious and numbers- and rules-oriented, you will be more successful in the burgeoning team-management mode if you learn from someone to be more social, playful, and flexible in your approach to interacting with others.

If you suffer from a lack of self-confidence, study the guy at the next workstation who seems to be brimming with self-confidence. Talk to him; ask questions. Find out how he does it. See if you can figure out how he talks to himself, on and off the job, and coaches himself into being confident. After all, that's what's behind the behavior we exhibit: We talk to ourselves. *"Inner talk" is extremely important.*

The flip side of the coin is that perhaps you need to *get away* from people who have been reinforcing your undesirable behavior patterns. If your mother is a worrier and you have inherited that trait, try to limit your visits with Mother. Otherwise, you may find that doing your filial duty may cost you more in lost sleep and aggravation than it's worth. If you tend toward gossip and back-stabbing and want to cure yourself of these workplace plagues, don't keep hanging out with gossipers and back-stabbers. Get some new friends, people who are more forgiving and positive about others.

Awareness of your need to sabotage yourself also will be the key to growth. Are you one of those people who needs to fail, to blow the opportunity that you fought to have, to orchestrate people and events so that you end up with a negative experience?

Use the Obstacles to Advance Your Goals

In the science of leadership, there is a primary operational principle that all leaders should know: *Always use your difficulties to advance your goals.*

To do this, it is necessary to learn to put yourself into whatever psychological state you wish to be in, regardless of the circumstances. Good leaders work on their inner leader so that whenever stress hits, their survival bag is full of techniques and skills to bail them out.

If you have cultivated your Leaderself, you will be able to will yourself into a safe space from which you can observe what is going on in front of or around you and choose whichever reaction will fit best. You learn how to shine a light on your internal emotional and intellectual makeup and become aware of yourself internalizing the external experience. Then you can decide to refrain from taking things so personally. Therefore, you stop being so reactive. You can actually lighten up.

Your Leaderself, you see, is powerful enough to over-come the instinctive internal emotional upheavals churned up by your Stress-self (from its connection to unresolved negative childhood experiences). Your bet-ter self will tell you, "You are more than just a little kid being automated into hurts or tirades by training and conditioning. You have a Leaderself and so you can re-channel emotions and create whatever reaction you want to in any given situation."

There will be many hindrances to your attempts to employ the primary operational principle of leadership. Your verbal brain, or ego, will start putting you down. You, however, can counter and talk back to that verbal brain. Tell it to "shut up!" as you have decided to build and rely upon another part of you, your Leaderself.

Put your awareness into positive thoughts and posi-tive images. Breathe in a natural and calm way. As your breathing continues steady and calm, the emotions that have welled up inside of you will subside. Then you also will find yourself relaxing physically, because your emo-tions are a subset of your physical being.

One instance where you can definitely implement the primary operational principle is during an encounter with an angry superior. One day you are sitting in your office doing fine and in storms your boss. He starts stomping around and erupts into criticisms of your work. Be aware of him, notice him, but don't believe you have to either shrivel up with fear or else respond by matching his bile.

If you have made a mistake, you might politely thank him for pointing it out and assure him it won't happen again. If you are being unjustly accused of something, you do not need to become defensive immediately. (Perhaps your boss wouldn't be in a mood to hear your defense anyway!)

The best way to appropriately use the primary operational principle is through meditation. Get into your safe space and then begin to call up uncomfortable images and situations. Rehearse in your Leaderself how you will deal with them when they occur. Train yourself to manage your feelings differently from what you've done before. Where once you would have exploded with anger, see yourself now as breathing through to a calmer state and producing a more thoughtful and measured response.

Your Leaderself, by the way, can even combat the ravages that your Stress-self put you through in the past. After getting into a comfortable, relaxed, focused state, you can evoke, one by one, painful experiences from years or months gone by. Then recreate how you behaved. Perhaps in one instance you stood at the deathbed of a close friend and acted like a marionette—no tears, just woodenly standing there—and then went home and put your fist through the wall. In your re-evocation you can let yourself feel and express your grief, allow yourself to tell the friend how much he or she meant to you, and go home and cry instead of the alternative.

Turn Negatives into Positives

Have you ever heard of "a double bind"? Usually we use this term as a negative—it's damned if you do and damned if you don't. Both options available to you point toward a bust.

Take a common workplace problem: One side of you wants to work 60, 70, 80 hours a week, advance, climb the ladder, bring home plenty of money. The other side of you wants to be at home with your wife and children, taking in ball games, throwing backyard parties, and generally enjoying family life.

If you satisfy the part that wants to do the workaholic number and get well fixed materially, you may jeopardize your relationships at home; you may even end up in divorce court. But if you go too far in the other direction, you fear you'll get passed over for promotions and never achieve your career goals.

The trick is to know how to turn a negative double bind (which is a lose/lose situation) into a positive double bind (a win/win situation).

The key is to state, then stay on *purpose* in both domains—at work and at home.

If your purpose at work is to achieve and advance, you'd be better advised to "work smart" rather than simply working long hours and courting burnout. Find ways to make much more efficient use of your time and energy. That way you can cut back from 70 hours a week to 55—and your wife (even though, ideally, she'd like you to put in only 40) will appreciate your efforts to switch more time to the family. Then when you're at home, focus on quality time with your spouse and children. Your kids won't be so glad you're home more if all you do is stay locked up in your basement workshop turning out pieces on your jigsaw or if you just pop in long enough to grab your golf clubs and say "sayonara." So put real energy into loving interactions with your family—following *their* interests and going places with *them*.

What you *don't* want to do, of course, is make it known that you're home to put in more quality time with your family and then let an afternoon or evening degenerate into squabbling. If that happens, you might just as well have stayed late at the office, right?

When you stay aware, however, even at the onset of a fight, you can turn negatives into positives. For one thing, you can swallow your anger as it starts to well up and sidetrack the argument before it gets started. The other positive thing you can do, should you happen to get into the fight anyway, is to stay aware and watch how you are channeling your anger and try to determine how you could rein in some of it so that your wife will no longer perceive you as Attila the Hun. The next time you get into a scrap with her, use what you've learned and make your behavior come out as more loving.

Pattern Intervention

Pattern intervention is an ideal technique for when you want to break up a nonproductive pattern of an individual or a group of employees. If an individual or group has been holding up a project or otherwise impeding progress, change the pattern.

When I do marriage counseling, frequently I'll find that both parties have been lying awake all night thinking about what they're going to say about the *other person's* disgraceful behavior.

The first time they come in, I encourage them to spill the junk about their mate. Sometimes, if I've seen them before in a self-awareness workshop, I already have a hunch what's coming. But the second time—or maybe even the first time if I think they have the awareness to handle it—I'll sit them down and ask, "Okay, who wants to start?" Usually the wife will volunteer. So I tell her, "What I'd like you to do now is give me your *husband's perspective* on why this marriage ended up here." Of course, then later I'll ask the husband to tell me why, *from his wife's point of view,* this marriage has gotten to a point of breakdown.

This tack immediately breaks the couple out of their egocentric mindsets. It strands them in right field. Suddenly they must learn the situation differently, give up their preconceived notions of how the counseling was going to go, and develop some sympathy for each other's perspectives.

A leader can do the same thing with his or her followers.

If, for instance, you see a rumble coming between two of your subordinates, call both of them in and ask them each to give *the other one's* perspective. You shouldn't do this until you have a fairly clear notion of what the passive aggressive or overtly confrontational pattern is in which they are caught up. Once you do, you can use pattern intervention to break them out of their mold.

The leadership motto for pattern intervention is: "Keep your eye on the target—but understand that there are a thousand different ways to hit it."

You know, there's only one mountain in front of you, but you get some mountain climbers together and they'll point out a number of different ways to scale it. If the path that you take runs into too much resistance or a threat beyond what you originally perceived was there, take another tack. If one of the techniques we're discussing here doesn't work well enough, please feel free to let go of it and move on to something else.

Placebo Strategy

If what you've been doing begins to stall, change it and do something different. This is the essence of the placebo strategy. Do you remember the Hawthorne experiment at Western Electric? In that experiment, Western Electric increased the lighting and changed the physical environment in a plant; the result was a big jump in productivity. Western Electric thought it was because it had improved the physical environment. Not exactly. Later, when Western Electric turned the lighting down and removed the soda vending machine, the company realized another jump in productivity. After the workers became habituated to the "new" conditions, however, productivity started to drop again.

Therefore, the lesson is that any change in your environment—whether your physical or your psychological environment—tends to produce a kick of energy.

There's a story I like about a rural Jewish community in the Middle East. In the community, there was a family: a husband with a wife, five children, and a mother-in-law who lives with them in their small three-bedroom house. Exasperated, the husband goes to the rabbi for counsel.

"My God, what I have to go through every day is awful. The kids are screaming, my wife is arguing with her mother all the time, and there's junk all over the place.

To act coolly, intelligently, and prudently in perilous circumstances is the test of a man—and also of a nation.

—Adlai E. Stevenson, Jr.

I'm about to lose my mind."

The rabbi just listens, then asks: "Do you own a goat?"

"Yes, I own a goat. I've got a goat in the shed outside. Why?"

"Bring the goat into the house," the rabbi says.

"WHAAAT! Are you crazy? Why would I want to bring the *goat* into the house? As if I didn't have enough trouble already!"

"Look, do you want my advice or not? You came to me as your rabbi and this is the advice I'm giving you. Take it or leave it."

Skeptical but obedient, the man goes home and moves the goat into the house.

Three days later he is back, beating on the rabbi's door. "Open up, open up, I've got to see you immediately!"

"What's the problem?" the rabbi inquires.

"It's that *goat!* The goat is dropping shit and pee all over the place. Nobody can keep up with it. And it moves around all night, bleating like a stuck pig, with the kids joining in to see who can bleat most like a goat, so nobody's sleeping—and this time I really *am* going to lose my mind. What do you recommend *now?*"

"Put the goat back in the shed," the rabbi says.

For Sabbath services the following week, the rabbi spots the man and says, "You didn't come back to report anything after my last advice. How are things going?"

"Oh, *much* better," the man says. "I'm sleeping again and there seems to be so much *room* in the house that we didn't have before."

Research on placebos shows that they work best with people in real pain, either physical or psychological or both. To combat pain, doctors sometimes try to provoke a new pain as a kind of placebo (putting the goat in the house). If it's to work, the new pain has to reach a certain threshold. When it gets there, it will trigger the endorphins and drive out the perception of the old pain.

Otherwise, placebos often are simply innocuous substances—sugar pills. The pill, however, is described as either a marvelous pain killer or else some other pharmaceutical that will bring relief. If the patient buys into this, the person's mind resets and releases endorphins in the brain. So simply creating a psychological expectation of good things can affect a change for the better in people's minds.

Perceptual Task Assignment

Traditional leadership centers on behavioral "task assignment." In other words, "Here's the job; go and do it!" For many managers, the beginning and end of their role is to assign tasks and then check the results. Perceptual task assignment goes considerably farther than that. It involves getting your people to see themselves and each other differently. You call upon employees to recreate themselves in ways that are useful for accomplishing the purposes and goals of their work assignment.

If someone is slow, he is called upon to recreate himself as working more rapidly. If someone is careless, he is challenged to learn how to be more attentive. Beyond that, they also are asked to develop a new vision of their colleagues—to see them as warmer, more competent, and more replete with productive possibilities than they had imagined before. After all, people tend to become the way others see them. We have plenty of anecdotal evidence, for instance, to support the notion that employees who are denigrated constantly will suffer even more lapses, and employees who are given encouragement and praise will improve their performance.

Ordeal Training

Ordeal training is boot camp. This is what collegians go through when they join a fraternity or a sorority. It's what happens in advanced self-awareness training.

Ordeal training is based on the idea that you can't fix something until you break it some more. There's a good medical analogy for this: a fracture. For example, when somebody is brought into the emergency room with a broken arm, the doctors sometimes must complete the break, make it a clean or thorough break, before they can set it properly to heal.

I won't work with anybody with addictions unless they first do our self-awareness workshop at Farr Associates. I don't want to waste my time and theirs. I want to make sure they've got the commitment and the guts to do what it will take to make them feel bad enough so that they will restructure their negative patterns. In the self-awareness workshop, we take a hairline fracture of a personality aberration and turn it into a complete break. Then, of course, we reset the fracture before the workshop concludes. In follow-up counseling, I can then nurture the healing process along.

The litmus test for whether somebody really wants to work on a problem is whether or not they'll do the self-awareness workshop. This is because the

Don't compromise yourself. You're all you've got.
—Janis Joplin

self-awareness workshop is tough. It cuts through people's defenses and barriers and opens up avenues into what's hurting inside of them. Many of us like to live in denial of the true sources of our dysfunctional behavior—such as addictive eating, working, smoking, drinking, or drug use. The workshop lays the sources bare—or at least it tries to. After people confront the hurting parts of themselves in the workshop, they are better prepared to make progress in counseling or some other recovery program.

Ordeal training also is done in the wilderness. Whitewater rafting is a venue. There you face raging water with dangerous situations all around, and you can't depend on your MBA or your VP nameplate or your stock options. You must find the best in your physical and emotional self and work to bring out the best in your raft mates.

Stress Interview

Have you ever heard of the "stress interview?" If you have a difficult and demanding task to assign to someone, bring the candidate in and put him or her through a battering ram kind of interview. You might sharply question their education or their job skills or even denigrate their family heritage. Really jerk them around. If they can survive the stress interview, they are a good bet to survive the brutal stress of a demanding project.

Part of the dynamic in ordeal training is that at first the candidate or subject is going to hate you. But if they want the payoff—a job assignment, healing, or a solution to some personal or professional quandary—badly enough, they will agree to go through the ordeal. At the end of the ordeal, if they have passed the test successfully, they will love you, and they'll follow you anywhere.

This phenomenon explains in part the bonding that takes place in college fraternities, military groups, and other groups that practice hazing as a condition of membership.

Reverse Psychology

Reverse psychology has its place, too, in the arsenal of leadership weapons.

I had a fellow in counseling once who was being hard on his body. Not only was he drinking, he also was smoking and overeating. One time he brought in a picture album about all his accomplishments in the military. In the album were medals and certificates of valor. I took the album from his hands and tossed it into the trash can. "This isn't you," I told him, pointing to the album. I had him look in a mirror: "This is you."

What's more, I told him that essentially he didn't have what it took to quit drinking, that, in fact, I expected him to go straight from our counseling session to a bar and drink. Well, he did go straight to a bar, but he so was angry with me that he ordered a ginger ale. This was a "psycho-logical" process I learned from Dr. Milton Erickson.

Milton Erickson, commonly known as "Uncle Miltie," was a master of reverse psychology. One time he was doing a lecture on hypnotherapy and a guy in the rear of the auditorium stood up and said, "This stuff is a fraud! And you're a liar!"

Uncle Miltie looked at him and shot back, "That's easy for you to say way back there in the crowd, but I bet you can't say that standing out in the aisle."

So the fellow got out in the aisle and repeated his accusation. Then Uncle Miltie said, "I bet you can't walk up to the front here and say that to my face."

Still angry, the man came up to Uncle Miltie and said, "You're a liar and this stuff's a fraud."

Uncle Miltie then challenged him again: "That's easy for you to say but I bet you can't sit down in that chair and go into a trance." The guy plopped into the chair and went out like a light.

CHAPTER ELEVEN

The True Leader Operates Out Of Purpose

IN THE LEADERSHIP PROCESS, you typically start with a notion of how *I* am going to get *them* to follow *me*. Of course, as those of you who have stayed with me thus far can clearly see, that is a myopic or at best a skewed approach to leading. Unless we are willing to get deeply into ourselves and confront the muck from our past that is fouling up the way we relate to people, we'll get nothing more than a superficial form of leadership stereotypes. These "skills" will hold up only until we're faced with a real crisis. At that point, our "leadership" will collapse in a pile of straw, the followers will walk out or walk all over us, the competition will move in and swipe our market share, and we may be so shaken we may never try to "lead" again.

Some of you sampling the content of this book may have gotten in touch with some fear. Apprehension. Anxiety. Self-doubt. "Just what would I be getting myself into if I tried to follow this Leaderself stuff?"

When people find themselves sent to our workshops at Farr Associates, they may put the question a bit differently (though it comes to the same thing): "I've got ten million things to get done this year and here I am taking off work days to come to this stupid workshop. Why are they making me do this? Am I that bad a manager? I thought I was doing a good job."

I tell the workshop participants, and I'm telling you right now, "Look, you can continue to operate out of your defense mechanisms, your Stress-self, or you can operate out of your purpose—which is to become a real leader."

If you choose the former, you will defend to the hilt, miss, obscure, or water down the message and go on being the same unaware manager you were before. Nothing will change in your relations to colleagues and subordinates. Though you may hold a position that carries authority and responsibility, you will fail to tap into and harness your hidden Leaderself. If you choose the latter purpose, you'll be willing to wince and take the hits to your ego that are necessary and move through the change process, even though it feels like walking through a wall of flames.

Intentions and purposes are often difficult to clarify for yourself as you try to bring forth your Leaderself. One reason is that at the outset, you may have persuaded yourself that your purpose was to "manage my time better" or "manage my people better." And all the while the *real* purpose was to better manage your own thoughts, perceptions, moods, reactions, and actions. That means, among other things, toning down or getting rid of your own maladaptive ways of responding to others, ways that are based in your *fears*. These include (but are not limited to) fear of: being wrong, being laughed at, failing, and being judged as "weak."

What's really important and the No. 1 way that leaders fail at their jobs is that they do not realize how controlling and how powerful are the frustrations, and behind those, the fear and the stress, that run their behavior. Once you succumb to your fears, they will organize your emotions and set you off on a course of action determined not by your Leaderself (the best of you) but by your Stress-self (the worst of you). Things then take shape all around you as a function of your giving in to fears and the temptation to defend yourself against all unwelcome criticism or embarrassment.

Speak to the Hump

As a leader you will have to shift back and forth between dealing with individuals and dealing with groups. This can mean knowing how to walk a tightrope.

Perhaps, in your best adaptive leader style, you have said one thing to Tom, something slightly different to Mary Lou, and something different again to Barney. Now how are you going to talk to the three of them—plus maybe eighteen others—as a group? By speaking to what I call "the hump."

In group leadership you want to speak to the needs and values of the whole group. Each group will develop its own personality, so that a group becomes almost like a new individual. Except that there are fringes to each group, militant enthusiasts on one side, dormant people on the other. In between there's quite a range, of course, but it can all be resumed in the overriding personality of the group formed by the middle. Learn to read both the fringes and the middle but speak to the middle of your group; that's "the hump."

Reading "the hump" requires every bit as much patience and intuition as does reading any one individual. You need all the openness to feedback that you can develop, and a good antennae for picking up on and responding to that feedback. Good teachers know how to speak to the hump and how to tone down the rebels on one fringe and wake up the sleepers on the other. (Teachers who don't possess these skills risk having the rebels turn other students against the teacher or else having the bulk of the class slide into sleep.)

Leading a group also can be compared to blazing a trail. The first time there's just underbrush and weeds to plow through. Nothing is clearly demarcated. The second time is already better. You can see where your first passage was because branches are bent out of your way and the undergrowth has been tamped down somewhat. After awhile, if you continue to use the same trail, you'll tame the forest floor. Now there's a path that invites a stroll, rather than a risky tromp through uncleared vegetation.

If you stop going down that trail, however, the undergrowth will swarm back and soon you'll be in raw wilderness again.

Turn into an Observer

To lead you also need a capacity to lay back and turn into an observer. The "observer" is the part of you that can be detached, or really, "non-attached." Pure observation, zero reaction. Passive, non-militant. Whatever's going on, you just stand there and watch it float by.

You'll especially need to rely on your observer side

when things are suddenly going into a tailspin—the boss's anger is out of control, conflict is erupting in your department, subordinates are resisting your leadership.

Restraining your inclination to react immediately is often a positive step. Instead, listen and try to assess what's going on.

Only after you believe you have heard enough to understand the scope of the problem can you begin to dig for the roots of the eruption or conflict. Not until you have gotten to what you believe to be the root of the matter, and only then, should you switch to a reactive mode.

(Even then, remember the caveat that the more resistance you perceive among your people, the greater is the need for you the leader to parry with an indirect approach to evoking effective followership.)

Workplace Relationships

When people utter the word "relationship," far more often than not they're talking about something romantic. Only infrequently do we stop to think that there's a kind of "romance" in any relationship. Thus do we speak of corporate mergers as courtship, "a good marriage," and all too often, a plunge toward breakup, or divorce.

People on the job have relationships too that contain elements of romantic couple matchups. Our interactions start with parrying, some wariness, gradual warming, then sometimes because of conflict or hurt feelings, a cooling

---

Managers do things right. Leaders do the right things.

—Warren Bennis

down and distancing phase. With skillful intervention by a leadership/relationships psychologist, a sort of "marriage counseling" can be brought to bear on weakened workplace relationships, and reconciliation can be facilitated.

To cite another example, a new employee might benefit from a six-week honeymoon with his or her superior and peers before a rougher reality sets in.

Good leaders recognize the highly personal dynamic in relationships in the plant or office. And getting these relationships to operate "in synch," especially at a deep level, is tricky.

Initially, workplace relationships tend to be pretty superficial. And in companies that prefer to operate in a state of low-grade awareness, human interactions often stay that way. Do you remember the scene in Woody Allen's movie *Annie Hall* when Woody is walking dolefully down the street just after his breakup with Annie? He's bemoaning to himself how love always seems to die and relationships end, and all of a sudden he spots the perfect all-American couple coming down the other side of the street.

The fellow looks like the captain of a college football team. He is right out of *GQ*—tall, blond, and ruggedly handsome. Beside him is the quintessential beauty queen, or head majorette. Virtually a *Vogue* cover girl. They are strolling hand in hand, obviously happy to be with each other.

Woody, intrigued, rushes up to them and blurts out: "It looks like you have the perfect relationship. How do you do it?"

The majorette type replies: "As long as we keep it completely superficial, it works just fine." Her GQ boyfriend nods in agreement.

Generally, that's the way the first phase of a relationship goes. I put my best foot forward, and you do, too, and we seem to hit it off great. I'm sensitive and caring; you're open and loving. And we see mainly each other's positives.

We're on our honeymoon, right?

Sooner or later, the bubble will burst. Maybe in one great explosion or gradually as the air or helium just seeps away until we feel as if we've been left with something flat and uninspiring.

That's when we start to run our games.

Leaders Know Their Games

"GAME" IS TRANSACTIONAL ANALYSIS TALK for manipulating another person. My own definition of a game is: what one person does to get himself hurt in such a way that he or she can blame the other party.

If you want to see what a game is actually like, get another person such as a coworker, your spouse, or a friend, and sit down next to one another. Now let's have one of you make a fist. The other person should now grasp that fist and use it to hit himself in the face. It's the other person's fist but you're using it to hit yourself. Got it? And now the person who's borrowed the fist should say to the owner of the fist, "You'd better stop hitting me. Otherwise, I'm gonna get angry! This is *your* fault. I'm not really doing this to myself. *You're the bad guy!*"

Gamesy, right? I organize all my feelings so that I can feel bad but I arrange to place the blame on *you*.

We know this happens in romantic relationships. We're less aware that the same dynamic is at work among people relating on the job. But it is. And it costs.

A company had a production problem. One unit of the

company had to buy parts from another unit for a manu-
facturing process, and somehow the orders were getting
gummed up. There never seemed to be enough parts
available from the supplying unit to meet the demand of
the purchasing unit.

Not atypically, the company had looked at all aspects of
the mechanical and financial systems but had failed to delve
into the human system: its own employee relationships. It
turned out that the head buyer and the head selling agent
from the two departments could not stand each other. So
in subtle and all-but-untraceable ways, the selling agent
had been sabotaging the process so that the other guy would
look bad. Exactly the kind of passive aggressive behavior
you often see in husband-wife relationships.

An associate of mine put the two supervisors through a
process of confrontation and awareness building and got
them to agree to act professionally for the benefit of the
company, overriding their bad feelings for one another.
Through a more in-depth and longer term process, the
consultant managed to get the two to work through their
hostilities and create a better relationship. If all this sounds
similar to marriage counseling, that's because it is.

Hostile feelings among coworkers, or between a superior and the troops, cause far more workplace problems
than generally is recognized. And unless you, the leader,
are in touch with your own feelings and have learned to
read feelings and attitudes of others, you are likely to
remain blind to what's wrong and how to fix it.

Persecutor, Victim & Rescuer

Of all the games we play in life, perhaps the most common is a triangle in which we alternate among the three
roles: Persecutor, Victim, and Rescuer.

Variations on this game are played out in office politics

in general, and during meetings in particular.

Imagine you are leading a meeting. Your boss, Susan, is in the room but is letting you handle the agenda. You make a strong point about the direction in which you feel the company should be moving, and lo, to your right flank, comes an attack! Jean, who's trying to gain recognition as a woman of original ideas and not a pat "yes-gal," contradicts your assertion and proposes a different course for the firm.

Assuming that she has ulterior motives, such as to move up in the company, she now commandeers the point on the triangle assigned to the persecutor. And you now assume the position of the victim.

Rescuers present at the meeting are going to speak up and bail you out, while those who feel like promoting Jean's persecutorial stance will side with her. This effectively splits the group into factions.

Noticing Susan's glance of strong permission for a defense, you decide to attack back and put Jean "in her place." If you do this with enough verbal punch, Jean now turns into the victim and you move up to the point occupied by the persecutor.

Bob, Ray, and others at the meeting may suddenly feel sympathy for Jean, as having been "unfairly maligned," and will rush to her rescue. Jean will pay them back in kind when they are under attack.

And around and around we go.

It should be obvious that many executive hours and talent are wasted in nonproductive game playing, which often does little to advance the mission of the company but focuses rather on individual one-upmanship.

A leader's role is to identify and short-circuit wasteful game playing and refocus everyone's attention on the mission and on the good of the company.

Why We Play Games

Game playing is driven by our Stress-self—that part of us that keeps telling us we're flawed or doomed to failure. Most of this part of us was formed by negative, belittling experiences in our childhoods.

To keep ourselves unaware of this dark cloud mushrooming inside of us, we create our "act," our front. And all of our games derive from our effort to maintain our act.

The paradox here is that whatever we avoid through playing our game we nonetheless end up becoming.

In other words, if you play a game to avoid rejection— such as when you reject them before they reject you— you still will end up feeling alone, unlovable, and rejected (and possibly guilty as well for behaving so deviously).

How Not to Play NIGYSOB

Let me add a note about one of the more insidious, and popular, games played in the work environment. It goes by the acronym of NIGYSOB, short for "Now I've Got You, S.O.B."

It takes two to play NIGYSOB: a conspiratorial persecutor and an unconsciously willing victim.

Let's say a supervisor, Jack, really dislikes a subordinate, Ralph. Jack asks his charge to complete a project single-handedly in three weeks. In reality, both parties realize that this is a mammoth job that ought to engage three people full-time for six weeks. But Ralph accepts the assignment without a peep. At the end of three weeks, of course, he has to confess to Jack that he's far from finished.

And Jack nails Ralph to the wall. Gotcha! NIGYSOB.

What game was Ralph playing? He moved into the victim's role and played a game called "Kick Me!" in which he allowed himself to be set up by his boss.

Ralph did have a choice; nothing but his own willingness to be victimized prevented him from refusing to take the bait of the impossible deadline. He could have said at the outset, "Look, Jack, if you think you can find somebody capable of delivering this project signed and sealed to you in three weeks, be my guest. Either give me some help or give me more time but what you're asking is really off the wall." But he didn't.

Nobody has to put himself in the victim position unless he has an unconscious need to be there. And some people do get a lot of mileage out of playing the unfairly put-upon. They get to trash their supervisors to other employees, wallow in self-pity, and otherwise moan and groan about management.

Victims Galore

Rescuers like to play a game called "Look How Hard I Tried" or else another one called "I Was Only Trying to Help." In each case they may end up failing—including failing to "save" someone else from his own incompetence. In some cases, a rescuer becomes a victim, especially when no one wants to take his or her advice.

In all cases, game players are trying to defend themselves against the surfacing of really bad vibes kicking around in their unconscious. It all boils down to (unconsciously) wanting to feel victimized, even when you play the persecutor's role.

A persecutor will justify his anger or his being overbearing by claiming, "You let me down! Why can't I depend on you?" In other words, "You are making me look bad if you don't do your job the way I want you to." Thus the persecutor gets to also be the victim.

End the Game with Self-Awareness

Jumping out of the circle of the game players demands awareness. Keen self-awareness.

The loser is a person who becomes so afraid that he allows his fear to run his being. The winner is afraid, too; but he gets beyond the fear, masters it, and stays in control of his thoughts and actions.

When someone tries to draw you into a game, you can react in one of two ways:

- You can go along and play—even though you suspect things will end badly.

- You can torpedo the game by refusing to play and creating a positive game.

For example, if a superior or a colleague criticizes you, you can decide not to take it personally. Let them say what they have to say; hear it out. That's where they are. Rather than attempting to blunt the criticism, just tell yourself, "This person has a need to be negative right now. I can just listen and decide later how to react in a way that serves my (and his true) purpose and goals."

Stay on Purpose

Stay on purpose. Is your purpose to get the job done or to win a personal tug-of-war with a boss or coworker?

Martin Luther King was a master at using other people's resistance to further his purpose. He allowed the racists to be racists while he continued to pursue equal rights for all. He refused to be trapped by the temptation to defend; and he used the tools of peaceful protest and powerful rhetoric rather than resorting to violence or ego games.

CHAPTER THIRTEEN

Conclusion

THIS BOOK HAS ATTEMPTED to present some break-through models and principles never presented before in terms of what it takes to be successful as a leader in America. It has attempted to illustrate and demonstrate why the most critical factor in the success or failure of a leader is not his intelligence, creativity, motivation, or how hard he or she works. Rather success or failure depends on how aware he or she is of the best of them and the worst of them (their unnecessary, self-limiting, negative outcome patterns).

After becoming aware of this fundamental recurring negative outcome pattern, the successful leader then develops strategies, techniques, and skills that are uniquely tailored to respond most effectively to this underlying pattern. Secondly, in order to get optimal leadership from the follower, the successful leader must apply the same process to his or her key followers, including the boss, key subordinates, and his or her spouse. Therefore, the leader must develop and use techniques that express his or her individual personality qualities and characteristics, and the leader also must develop and modify unique techniques to deal with unique, individual followers.

The leader has the expectation that meaningful change in personality as well as overt behavior is not only possible, but inevitable. The successful leader knows that growth and development are the process of living, and poor followership is an interference with that process. Thus, when the leader sees poor followership on the part of the follower, the first responsibility of the successful leader is to accept what the follower offers, including pessimism, resistance, rigid thinking patterns, or overt behavior patterns. The successful leader then, with an emphasis on the range of possibilities, explores with the follower all the different possibilities for solutions to these patterns. The successful leader is willing to take responsibility and make decisions for the follower if that is necessary, and understands that each case is handled individually and uniquely, depending on the follower.

The leader is not concerned with the "roots" of poor followership behavior. He or she just views it as an inappropriate functioning to be corrected. To this end, he or she might block the malfunctioning pattern either by relabeling the pattern, by taking it over and changing it under direction, or by providing an ordeal that makes it

The worst leaders get hardening of the categories and simply get older, meaner, more vindictive, and more cruel. The best leaders also get older as well as wiser, more compassionate with others and themselves, and more truly loving of their followers.

Conclusion

You Make the Music

➣ *Your job now, to one degree or another, is to conduct a symphony orchestra and make beautiful music—having it all blend. Instead of flying solo, being out there playing the drums or blowing a horn. The way you got where you are is because you were good at providing drums or blowing a horn, but that isn't what it takes for you to be successful or effective as a leader. To do that you need to learn to conduct the orchestra.*

difficult to continue the pattern. The leader then creates a strong, intense relationship with the follower and uses the relationship to get the follower to cooperate or appropriately rebel. The leader will use the likes and dislikes, analogies, stories, and life experiences of the follower to create meaningful interactions and appropriate followership from the follower.

Thus, the focus of the leadership-followership relationship is on the present and on the interaction patterns both within the leader, within the follower, and between the leader and the follower. An assumption is that the follower is doing the best that he or she can do under the circumstances, and that negative follower interactions are simply ways the follower is attempting to communicate to the leader.

Therefore, the leader has a present or future time orientation, and has a recognition, acceptance, and participation by the leader of all levels of the followers' behavior in communication. The leader understands that there is no requirement that the leader change his or her inner experience, values, principles, needs, or feelings, but in order to improve the followership responsiveness, the leader is required to change his or her overt behavior, what he or she says or doesn't say, does or doesn't do.

The most successful leaders in a relatively free market economy in a democratic cultural environment understand that they do not come out of their inner needs, feelings, values, or principles. Within an appropriate ethical, moral, and legal framework, the successful leader in a democratic environment comes out of the needs, feelings, and personality maps of the follower. Thus, the only limit to powerful, charismatic, effective leadership is how creative and versatile a leader is in his or her verbal and physical behavior, and how aware and observant the leader is in applying his or her awareness, understanding, and skills.

It is my hope and intention that this book has provided food for thought and action in your journey to the next level in your leadership path.

Index

Index

Plaques, Cards, Books, and Tapes from

Andrews-Speed Publications

Plaques

Awareness Plaques

Remind yourself on a daily basis of the principles and processes of Tony Speed's awareness workshops. These awareness plaques express principles and processes that are taught in the awareness workshops. (Printed on parchment paper and mounted in a sturdy acrylic stand / $18.00)

Awareness Plaque #1

Side one - Rejection Doesn't Exist

Side Two - Relationships

Awareness Plaque #2

Side One - I Like You

Side Two - Dance to the Music

Awareness Plaque #3

Side One – Love and Loving

Side Two – To Love Yourself

Teamleaderself Plaque

Teamleaderself Principles and Practices Plaque. Remind yourself and others of these 14 principles and practices that form the foundation for appropriate and powerful leadership. Printed on gold parchment paper and mounted in a sturdy acrylic stand, these helpful reminders can be displayed attractively throughout the workplace. (Two-sided stand is 8½" X 11" in size / $18.00)

Book and Tape Sets

The Relationship Roller Coaster Book and Tape Set

The Relationship Roller Coaster: Riding Out the Ups and Downs helps you focus on the mechanics, elements, and processes you need to master to keep your relationships on track. This book and tape set helps you understand and develop both your personal and professional relationships. (176-page paperback and 4 audio tapes / $50.00)

Living, Loving & Laughing Book and Tape Set
Living, Loving and Laughing: A Guide to Self-Awareness is a practical, how-to guide for having it all; for achieving self-awareness and applying it to your ordinary world. Anthony Andrews-Speed, who has a Ph.D. in psychology, helps you:
- Discover purpose in your life
- Build relationships instead of entanglements
- Move through body blocks and barriers to awareness
- Live, love and laugh as if your life depends on it

(160-page paperback and 4 audio tapes / $50.00)

Meditations Book and Tape Set
Meditations, Contemplations & Visualizations is chocked full of narratives, guided meditations, contemplations, and visualizations (not to mention terrific graphic art work by Mary Pugh) for expanding your intuitive, creative power, and sensitivity. This book and tape set is designed to be read and heard, not only with the eyes and ears, but also with the heart. The tape set includes two peaceful way and two powerful way training tapes. (256-page paperback and 4 audio tapes / $50.00)

Awareness Cards

These greeting cards —or Awareness Cards—contain poems and expressions from the experience and understanding of those who attended Tony Speed's Self-Awareness workshops. The cards, which are printed on recycled paper in the popular environmental color of terra flax, are available in sets of eight. Matching envelopes are provided. (Set of eight cards / $18.00)

Andrews-Speed Publications Order Form

_____Awareness Plaques and Teamleadership Principles and Practices Plaque (Plaque / $18.00)

_____The Relationship Roller Coaster: Riding Out the Ups and Downs (Book / $14.95)

_____The Relationship Roller Coaster (Book and Tapes / $50.00)

_____Living, Loving and Laughing: A Guide to Self-Awareness (Book / $14.95)

_____Living, Loving and Laughing: A Guide to Self-Awareness (Book and Tapes / $50.00)

_____Meditations, Contemplations & Visualizations (Book / $14.95)

_____Meditation, Contemplations & Visualizations (Book and Tapes / $50.00)

_____Tony Speed's Awareness Cards (8 cards per set) (Cards / $14.00)

_____Subtotal

_____NC Residents add 6% sales tax

_____Shipping & Handling (see instructions below)

_____Total Enclosed

Name _____

Address _____

City _____ State _____

Zip _____

Mail your order with payment to:
Anthony Andrews-Speed, Ph.D.
Farr Associates, Inc.
4524 W. Wendover Avenue
Greensboro, NC 27409

Shipping Information
Please include $2.50 shipping and handling for your first two books, individual tapes or card sets. Add $1.00 for each additional item. Shipping and handling for a tape series or book/tape combination is $3.00 each. Orders shipped to North Carolina addresses must include 6% sales tax.